THE ISLAMIC CONQUESTS IN EUROPE

The Islamic Conquests in Europe

GEW SOCIAL SCIENCES GROUP

Copyright © 2025 by GEW Social Sciences Group
Series: Swords of Faith
Global East-West (London)
All rights reserved. No part of this book may be reproduced in any
manner whatsoever without written permission except in the case of
brief quotations embodied in critical articles and reviews.
First Printing, 2025

Contents

1	Introduction	1
2	Islamic conquests in Europe	19
3	Overview of Key Questions and Puzzles	37
4	The Conquest of Spain	57
5	Expansion into Southern France	75
6	The Byzantine Front: the Balkans and Greece	91
7	The Siege of Constantinople	105
8	The Legacy of Islamic Rule in Europe	123
9	Cultural Exchange and Integration	137
10	Economic Impact and Trade	149
11	Religious Shifts and Interactions	165
12	Military Strategies and Tactics	181
13	Legacy and Memory	197
14	Summary of key findings	209
15	Reflections on significance	227
	Bibliography	243

Chapter 1

Introduction

Contextualising the Islamic Conquests in Europe

The Islamic conquests in Europe remain one of history's most transformative and multifaceted episodes, dramatically altering the region's trajectory (Kennedy, 2004). To fully grasp their significance, one must look beyond the victories and borders to the intricate historical context that fostered such sweeping change. These events were not isolated; they emerged from an intricate web of political disarray, cultural shifts, and religious developments that predated them (Crone, 2005).

Before the dawn of the Islamic conquests, Europe was a fractured mosaic of kingdoms, tribal societies, and waning empires (Hodgson, 1974). The once-mighty Roman Empire, long a unifying force, had by the 7th century devolved into its Eastern Byzantine remnant—still formidable, yet beleaguered by internal instability and external aggressors (Brown, 1989). This fragmentation left a patchwork of opportunities across Europe, ripe for exploitation by emerging powers (Robinson, C., 2011).

Simultaneously, a transformative spiritual and political movement was sweeping out of the Arabian Peninsula. The rise of Islam under the Prophet Muhammad introduced a fresh cultural and ideological paradigm to the ancient world (Eisenstadt,

1986). The rapid expansion of the early Islamic community, crystallised politically in the Caliphate, reshaped territories that had long been dominated by the Byzantine and Sassanian empires (Lapidus, 1988). This surge extended far beyond the Middle East, setting the stage for the conquests that followed in Europe (Hawting, 2000).

The Islamic forces, propelled by both political pragmatism and religious fervour, challenged Europe's entrenched powers. Responses to this new reality varied—from outright resistance to strategic alliances, even occasional accommodation (Kennedy, 2004). For the Byzantine Empire, positioned at the crossroads of East and West, these conquests presented an existential threat. They faced waves of incursions while grappling with their own dwindling resources and internal divisions (Howard, 2001).

Amid this shifting landscape of rivalries, allegiances, and territorial upheavals, the Islamic campaigns into Europe unfolded. These conquests were not merely military ventures but multidimensional crusades imbued with strategic precision and a spiritual imperative. Muslim forces, driven by the concept of spreading the *Dar al-Islam* (the Abode of Islam), sought to introduce new lands to the teachings of Islam while consolidating their territorial foothold (Bennison, A.K., 2009).

To truly contextualise the Islamic conquests in Europe, one must see them as the culmination of broader historical trends. The interplay of economic motives, political fragmentation, and religious mission created fertile ground for the emergence of a new chapter in European history—one that would reverberate across centuries (Ibn Khaldun, 1998).

The Historical Backdrop of the Conquests

Far from being isolated flashpoints of history, the Islamic conquests in Europe were deeply interwoven with a web of antecedent developments that set the stage for their success (Shaban, 1970). The roots of these campaigns stretched back to the origins of Islam itself, with the nascent Muslim community rapidly growing in both spiritual conviction and geopolitical ambition following the Prophet Muhammad's teachings (Hourani, A., 1991).

The death of Muhammad in 632 AD did not weaken this momentum; rather, it marked the beginning of determined expansion under the first four Caliphs of the Rashidun era. These leaders launched campaigns to spread Islamic principles, assert Muslim authority, and secure economic and territorial gains. This combination of spiritual mission and political strategy proved a potent formula for expansion, forging an empire that would soon encroach upon Europe's borders (Riley-Smith, 2000).

One of the central motivators behind these campaigns was the early Muslim community's profound commitment to spreading monotheism and establishing social justice as prescribed by Islamic doctrines. They saw themselves as agents of transformation, tasked with building a morally guided society unified under the banner of Islam (Berkey, J., 2003). This fervent belief in their role, coupled with pragmatic efforts to consolidate power, spurred the Muslim armies to advance into territories long dominated by mighty civilisations like the Byzantines and Sassanians (Lapidus, 1988).

The timing of these conquests was critical. The Byzantine and Sassanian Empires, after decades of exhausting warfare against one another, were severely weakened ((Haldon, J., 2010)). Their fractured defences and diminished capacities created a window of opportunity for the Arab-Islamic forces. Capitalising on this moment of decline, the Muslim armies turned formidable opponents into conquered territories, capturing key regions in the Fertile Crescent, North Africa, and ultimately Europe (Crone, 2005).

As the Arab forces surged into lands such as Syria, Egypt, and Iraq, they encountered civilisations rich in culture, resources, and infrastructure. Rather than pursuing wholesale destruction, they often absorbed and adapted to the existing systems, integrating these territories into the rapidly expanding Islamic empire (Kennedy, 2004). These strategic gains served as invaluable stepping stones for their ventures into Europe, linking military success with economic viability (Hawting, 2000).

What emerged was a coordinated effort that combined spiritual zealotry with calculated pragmatism. Europe became an arena where the Islamic empire sought to assert dominance not only by force but through cultural exchange, economic integration, and religious outreach. The backdrop of these conquests—a world marked by political disunity, ideological transformation, and resource-driven ambition—underscores their profound significance in shaping the contours of European history (Shaban, 1970).

The Complex Tapestry of "Islamic Conquests": Definition and Extent

When we speak of the term **"Islamic conquests"**, we delve into an era of dramatic political, cultural, and territorial transformations. Historically, this phrase references a sweeping series of military campaigns led by Muslims during the early Middle Ages (Hodgson, 1974). Far more than just an assemblage of battles, these conquests signalled the rapid extension of Islamic power from the core of the Arabian Peninsula outward, engulfing regions previously dominated by disparate cultures, religions, and political systems (Haldon, J., 2010).

The scope of these conquests was astonishing in scale. **From the sunlit coasts of the Iberian Peninsula (modern Spain and Portugal) to the vibrant cities of the Byzantine Empire, and as far as Southern France, Italy, and the Balkans**, Islamic forces surged across borders, reshaping entire civilisations (Kennedy, 2004). This expansion disrupted the existing balance of power in Europe, leaving far-reaching impacts on the continent's political, cultural, and religious evolution (Robinson, C., 2011).

FORCES DRIVING THE ISLAMIC CONQUESTS

The motivations behind this vast expansion were varied and multifaceted. Chief among them was the desire to **propagate Islam**, a faith that saw itself not only as a spiritual guide but also as a political force (Berkey, J., 2003). The unification of the Arabian Peninsula under the banner of Islam created a thirst to **extend the caliphate's influence**, subsuming territories, peoples, and material wealth in the process. Muslim armies distinguished themselves with innovative tactics, superior weaponry, and charismatic leadership, enabling swift victories and consolidation of power (Howard, 2001).

Yet, these conquests were not pursued in isolation—contacts between newly Islamic regions and the broader world facilitated a **dynamic exchange of knowledge, governance systems, and cultural expressions**, as Arabic language and Islamic frameworks took root in conquered lands (Lapidus, 1988).

THE IMPACT: TRANSFORMATION AND RESISTANCE

The transformation wrought by these conquests was profound. On the one hand, **new political entities emerged**, governed by Sharia law and underpinned by Islamic administrative structures. On the other, Arabic culture and the Islamic arts flourished, enriching conquered lands and forging enduring legacies. Indeed, the conquests acted as a channel for the transfer of ideas—science, art, literature, and philosophy being the most notable—between the Islamic world and Europe (Bennison, A.K., 2009).

Despite these successes, resistance was a constant thread in the story of the Islamic conquests. Indigenous populations, as well as rival powers, mounted defence after defence, their cultural identities persevering in the face of change (Goldziher, 1971). This tension underscores the complex, multifaceted legacy of the conquests—a legacy still keenly relevant in discussions of European and Islamic relations today (Ibn Khaldun, 1998).

Targets of Islamic Conquests: Strategic Calculations

The ambitions of the Islamic conquerors were meticulously focused. **Regions of cultural, economic, and political significance became prime targets**, as Muslim forces sought to cement their influence in places of strategic importance (Haldon, J., 2010).

THE IBERIAN PENINSULA: A PRIZE OF RICHES AND POSITION

A key area affected was the Iberian Peninsula. In 711 CE, led by Tariq ibn Ziyad, Muslim forces crossed the Strait of Gibraltar, embarking on a campaign that swiftly dismantled the **Visigothic Kingdom of Hispania** (Kennedy, 2004). More than its fertile lands, the peninsula's geopolitical importance made it an irresistible target. It wasn't by chance that **Al-Andalus**, established by the Umayyads, became a flourishing hub of culture and innovation. Remarkably, Muslim rule in Spain endured for centuries, leaving behind architectural marvels, intellectual advancements, and an indelible mark on its identity (Lapidus, 1988).

SICILY AND SOUTHERN ITALY: CONTROLLING THE MEDITERRANEAN

The conquest of **Sicily and Southern Italy** followed in the 9th century, when Muslim control extended not only across the island but to crucial coastal enclaves in the region (Howard, 2001). Sicily's **prime location within the Mediterranean** was a boon to Muslim fleets, empowering them to dominate **sea trade routes** and enhance cultural and economic connections (Robinson, C., 2011). Moreover, a Muslim presence in Southern Italy catalysed interactions across diverse societies—a theme that would become characteristic of Islamic occupation.

SOUTHERN FRANCE: STRAINS AGAINST THE FRANKS

Another focal point was France, particularly its southern regions. While the eventual Frankish resistance—led by Charles Martel—halted further Muslim advance into Western Europe at the **Battle of Tours in 732 CE**, the invasion served as a monumental moment in shaping long-term European-Islamic dynamics (Goldziher, 1971).

THE BYZANTINE EMPIRE: AN ENDURING CHESSBOARD

The Byzantine Empire, another formidable target, became a frontline battlefield for the Islamic conquests. Campaigns infiltrated heartland territories like Thessalonica and Corinth, weakening Byzantine defences and creating Muslim footholds (Crone, 2005). Major sieges in 717–718 and again in 860–861 underscored both the ambition of the caliphates and the resilience of Byzantium. These encounters entrenched the empire and its neighbours as central players in the ongoing struggle (Ibn Khaldun, 1998).

MOTIVATIONS: FAITH, WEALTH, AND OPPORTUNITY

What compelled such relentless waves of expansionism? The motivations underlying the conquests were a layered amalgamation of faith, ambition, and opportunity. Islamic principles such as **jihad**, interpreted broadly to include territorial expansion, spurred Muslim forces to spread what they considered to be divine governance (Howard, 2001). This spiritual ambition was matched by material incentives, with Europe's fertile lands, abundant resources, and established trade routes offering compelling rewards for invaders (Shaban, 1970).

Additionally, disarray within Europe itself further emboldened campaigns. **Internal divisions, fragmented political systems**, and weakened governing bodies across key regions only hastened the ease of Islamic incursions. Their capacity to exploit these fissures laid the groundwork for wide-ranging conquests and enduring rule.

The European Political Aftermath

The political ripples of the Islamic conquests reshaped Europe in often unpredictable ways. Entire regions were absorbed into **a vast Islamic empire**, altering the geopolitical and cultural fabric of the continent (Riley-Smith, 2000). Alongside territorial integration came the **implementation of Sharia-based governance**, which redefined the administrative and social frameworks of the conquered lands (Goldziher, 1971).

Post-conquest, Europe found itself faced with novel political realities. **Diplomatic engagements emerged across Islamic and Christian spheres**, characterised by uneasy truces, alliances, and outright hostilities. Whether trading goods or clashing on battlefields, these entanglements formed the basis for centuries of complex interaction—interactions that would simultaneously divide and unite the continents (Eisenstadt, 1986).

The "Islamic conquests" were more than a sequence of military campaigns. They were transformative episodes enriched by religious zeal, political opportunism, and cultural exchange. In targeting strategic regions and reshaping vast portions of Europe, these conquests left behind legacies of innovation, interaction, and resistance. Though resistance to Islamic rule ensured the survival of indigenous traditions and governments, the conquests irreversibly altered the trajectory of European history. Whether through architecture, governance, intellectual fervour, or the simple legacy of shared spaces, Islam's imprint on medieval Europe reverberates to this day.

These exchanges had long-term social implications, forging hybrid identities and fostering a cultural connectivity that transcended borders. Kennedy (2004) observes that the flow of ideas, art, science, and commerce between Islamic and European civilisations facilitated mutual enrichment, leaving a shared legacy visible in fields as diverse as architecture, medicine, and philosophy. The Islamic conquests, therefore, were not a one-sided imposition but a dynamic interaction that redefined the social fabric of regions under their influence.

Politically, Hodgson (1974) identifies the conquests as pivotal in altering Europe's power dynamics. Islamic rule introduced new methods of statecraft, diplomacy, and legal administration, reshaping the political landscape of the Mediterranean world. This created spaces for innovative governance models, some of which influenced the trajectories of emerging European polities. Haldon, J. (2010) points out how the presence of Islamic polities in Europe forced neighbouring civilisations to adapt, spurring changes in military strategy, economic policy, and interregional diplomacy. Beyond immediate impacts, these changes laid the foundations for enduring political transformations.

Ibn Khaldun (1998) provides a broader perspective, noting that these conquests catalysed a dynamic interplay of forces—conflicts and collaborations—that shaped the narrative of European history. The legacy of Islamic rule in Europe remains not just a history of conquest but a period of profound socio-political transformation, one characterised by both tensions and syntheses that defined a new era in global history.

The religious and cultural dynamics, challenges, and legacy of the Islamic conquests in Europe present a rich and intricate tapestry of historical development, marked by diverse interactions, obstacles, and enduring contributions that shaped the trajectory of European history.

RELIGIOUS AND CULTURAL DYNAMICS

The Islamic conquests introduced a multifaceted interplay of faiths and traditions across Europe, catalysing periods of contestation, collaboration, and cultural exchange. The Muslim forces encountered and governed regions inhabited by Christians, Jews, and occasionally pagans, fostering both tensions and cooperation. This interplay exemplifies the pluralistic governance strategies characteristic of Islamic rulers.

Under Islamic rule, *dhimmi* policies—granting People of the Book (Christians and Jews) the right to maintain their faiths in exchange for taxation via the *jizya*—served as a functional mechanism for coexisting with diverse religious communities (Kennedy, 2004). This dynamic created an environment where religious autonomy was permitted, albeit under Islamic dominance, allowing cultural and intellectual heterogeneity to flourish.

Intriguingly, cultural interactions surpassed mere coexistence. The Islamic conquests facilitated a vibrant exchange of ideas: Islamic scholars preserved and expanded upon ancient Hellenistic knowledge, making significant advancements in fields like philosophy, mathematics, and medicine before reintroducing these works to Europe during its own intellectual awakening (Lapidus, 1988). Similarly, forms of European artistic, linguistic, and culinary traditions interacted with Islamic culture, showcasing mutual influence born of conquest and proximity.

Despite this intellectual osmosis, religious differences often ignited conflict. Throughout the conquests, institutions like the Christian Church viewed Islam as both a military and theological threat, exacerbating tensions. Periodic uprisings and resistance to Islamic governance often stemmed from efforts by conquered populations to reclaim sovereignty over religious and cultural identity (Haldon, J., 2010).

CHALLENGES FACED BY ISLAMIC FORCES

The Islamic forces faced profound challenges as they pushed into European territory. Logistical difficulties were significant: campaigns stretched across vast landscapes, often into regions with rugged terrain and unfamiliar climates. Maintaining lines of communication, rebuilding armies, and ensuring supply chains across an expanding frontier tested the limits of resource management (Shaban, 1970).

Resistance from entrenched European powers posed another formidable obstacle. The Byzantine Empire, with its established military infrastructure and strategic fortifications, mounted significant resistance (Crone, 2005). Even after notable victories, such as the conquest of Visigothic Spain, organised Christian monarchies and coalitions like the Reconquista spearheaded by northern Iberian kingdoms gradually began reversing Islamic territorial gains.

Furthermore, internal divisions occasionally hindered Islamic advancement. Rivalries within the Caliphates or leadership disputes over regional sectors weakened operational unity. Simultaneously, differing cultural and religious customs between the Arab, Berber and other Muslim contingents sometimes hampered cohesion within the conquest forces themselves (Kennedy, 2004).

LEGACY IN SHAPING EUROPE'S DEVELOPMENT

The legacy of the Islamic conquests in Europe is diverse and profound. Islamic rule, particularly in regions like Al-Andalus (present-day Spain and Portugal), acted as a bridge between the ancient world and medieval Europe, transferring critical knowledge through the translated works of Greek philosophers like Aristotle and scientific treatises from Persia and India (Hodgson, 1974).

This intercultural exchange laid the groundwork for the Renaissance, a period that revolutionised European art, philosophy, and science. For instance, Islamic advancements in algebra (a term itself derived from Arabic), optics, and medicine served as foundational pillars for Europe's subsequent scientific revolution (Haldon, J., 2010). Universities, such as those in Córdoba and Toledo, became renowned centres for intellectual collaboration.

Architectural and artistic legacies also endure. The iconic horseshoe arch and vibrant geometric designs introduced by Islamic builders during their tenure in Europe influenced Gothic and Romanesque architectural styles. One only must look at structures like the Great Mosque of Córdoba or the Alhambra to witness the enduring beauty of this period's artistic synthesis.

At the linguistic level, Arabic enriched European vernaculars through words related to science (*algebra*, *alchemy*), agriculture (*sugar*, *saffron*), and trade (*tariff*, *admiral*), marking a subtle but significant imprint on the continent's languages (Riley-Smith, 2000).

Lastly, the Islamic conquests also shaped Europe's cultural identity by providing a "civilisational other." The complex confrontation and interchange between Islamic and Christian traditions defined much of Europe's self-perception regarding religion, governance, and cultural destiny. Even as Islamic rule waned in regions like Iberia, the legacy of this era echoed through residual cultural practices, diplomatic policies, and the shared history of Mediterranean civilisations.

In summary, through the religious and cultural dynamics they introduced, the challenges they navigated, and the intellectual and artistic advancements they catalysed, the Islamic conquests in Europe remain pivotal in understanding the continent's historical and cultural evolution. These encounters not only facilitated cross-cultural exchanges that enriched humanity's collective knowledge but also forged enduring legacies that continue to influence the global cultural and scientific narrative today.

The study of the Islamic conquests in Europe holds immense significance in understanding the broader arc of European history, primarily because these conquests serve as a lens through which one can examine the transformative processes of intercultural interaction, knowledge exchange, and political restructuring.

CULTURAL AND INTELLECTUAL CONTRIBUTIONS

The Islamic conquests facilitated a dynamic transfer of knowledge and innovation that shaped Europe's intellectual evolution. During this period, Islamic scholars preserved, enhanced, and transmitted knowledge that would later spark significant advancements in Europe. For instance, works of Greek philosophers and scientists were preserved and expanded upon in the Islamic world and then reintroduced to Europe, laying the foundation for the Renaissance (Kennedy, 2004; Riley-Smith, 2000). Additionally, innovations in mathematics, astronomy, medicine, and architecture enriched European societies. Notably, the influence of Moorish architecture and agricultural techniques in areas such as Al-Andalus (modern-day Spain) demonstrated the tangible impact of Islamic rule on European culture.

RELIGIOUS AND SOCIETAL TRANSFORMATIONS

The introduction of Islam into Europe via conquest altered the continent's religious and societal composition. While regions such as Spain experienced centuries of Islamic governance, these periods fostered environments where diverse religious groups – Muslims, Christians, and Jews – coexisted to varying degrees, leading to cultural syncretism. The convivencia (coexistence) of Al-Andalus illustrates how Islamic rule catalysed the blending of traditions, even as it also sparked religious tensions and resistance (Hawting, 2000). Such tensions would culminate in events like the Reconquista, the later religious unification of Spain, and a reshaped Christian identity in Europe.

POLITICAL AND MILITARY IMPACT

The Islamic conquests disrupted and restructured European power dynamics. The initial waves of conquests introduced a formidable new political force to the Mediterranean world, challenging long-established powers such as the Byzantine Empire. In Spain, the establishment of Muslim rule under the Umayyads transformed the regional political landscape, ushering in centuries of Islamic governance that would only give way to Christian rule after protracted and interwoven military campaigns (Shaban, 1970; Howard, 2001). Moreover, the presence of Islamic empires prompted defensive alignments and conflicts that shaped European unity, particularly in response to shared threats like the advance of the Ottoman Empire in later centuries.

BROADER HISTORICAL RELEVANCE

In addition to their immediate effects, the Islamic conquests encapsulate broader lessons about the interconnectedness of world history. They demonstrate that Europe's development was not an isolated process but part of a larger, global narrative involving exchanges and conflicts across Africa, Asia, and the Middle East (Eisenstadt, 1986). The nuanced analysis of these conquests encourages historians to reject overly simplistic or monolithic narratives, instead adopting a more integrative approach that accounts for intercultural exchange, adaptation, and resistance.

Ultimately, the study of the Islamic conquests challenges static views of European history by foregrounding the dynamic and reciprocal relationships that shaped the continent's trajectory. It illuminates how Europe, far from being a closed cultural sphere, was part of a wider network of civilisations whose interactions profoundly influenced its political, intellectual, and cultural evolution. In this way, the Islamic conquests form an essential chapter in unpacking the multifaceted history of Europe.

Chapter 2

Islamic conquests in Europe

Background of the Islamic Expansion

The dawn of Islam in the 7th-century Arabian Peninsula heralded a seismic shift in history, birthing a powerful movement of faith, conquest, and empire-building. The Prophet Muhammad's message—a blend of spiritual revelation and social reform—resonated widely, unifying fragmented tribes and herding them from internal feuding to a collective purpose (Esposito, 1998). What started as a regional phenomenon soon spilled beyond Arabia's arid heartlands, driven by a nexus of religious zeal, political calculation, and economic opportunity (Fierro, M. 2005).

The death of the Prophet transitioned leadership to the early caliphs, who assumed the dual mantle of spiritual and political authority. These successors viewed expansion not merely as a consequence of faith but as a purposeful strategy to cement Islam's place on the global stage (Lambton, 1988). At the core of this mission lay a profound conviction: that Islam's teachings must extend far and wide, guiding other societies towards submission to the divine will of Allah (Ibn Khaldun, 1990). For many early Muslims, conquest was perceived as an act of duty—a sacred obligation to spread their burgeoning monotheistic vision (Seddon, 2012).

Yet alongside the spiritual drive were unflinching political ambitions. The caliphs understood that territorial acquisition bolstered prestige, subdued rival powers, and stabilised internal authority (Robinson, 2011). The Islamic empire grew not only from the fervour of belief but also through the shrewd pragmatism of empire-building. Furthermore, economic motivations surged alongside piety and politics. The allure of controlling trade routes, harnessing agricultural riches, and extracting valuable resources invigorated the impulse for conquest (Ayalon, 1989). Lands like North Africa offered fertile plains, bustling commercial hubs, and strategic positions poised between East and West, making them an irresistible prize.

As the Islamic armies marched into North Africa, they met a mosaic of cultures, from Berber tribes' fiercely independent pastoralists to faltering Byzantine outposts and vestiges of Roman influence (Brett & Fentress, 1996). Such diversity did more than complicate conquest—it influenced the course of Islamic history itself, shaping the evolving empire. The fusion of faith, power, and economic aspirations created an unstoppable wave, ushering in an era of transformation. This confluence of forces laid the foundation for an empire that would leave an indelible mark on world history, catalysing shifts across continents, cultures, and centuries (Holt, 2006).

Initial Conquests in North Africa

The tide of Islamic conquest swept into North Africa with energy and inevitability, altering the region in ways few could have foreseen. Beginning under the Rashidun Caliphate in the mid-7th century, Arab forces embarked on a campaign that would reconfigure the political, social, and cultural landscape of the Western world (Kennedy, 2004). Commanded by figures of legendary reputation, like Uqba ibn Nafi and Abdullah ibn Saad, the Muslim armies moved with speed and coordination that left their adversaries reeling (Kennedy, H. 2007). Across harsh deserts and winding coastal paths, their pursuit of victory was relentless—a calculated dance of strategy and improvisation.

One of the earliest and most decisive triumphs came at the Battle of Sufetula in 647. The Byzantines, caught unprepared, were crushed by Arab forces who claimed a vital foothold in Tunisia. This victory shattered resistance and unleashed further advances westward into Libya and Egypt, pulling these lands into the increasingly vast fold of the Caliphate (Gibb, 1969). Yet, progress was far from effortless. Complex terrains and fragmented alliances among local Berber tribes presented formidable challenges. The Berbers, known for their defiance, engaged in fierce resistance, forcing the Arab armies to adapt their strategies repeatedly (Hourani, A. 2010).

Against these odds, unity and determination prevailed. The Arab forces, united by a cause larger than mere conquest, supplanted fragmented opposition with administrative systems that transformed the conquered territories. They established garrisons and governance centres designed to anchor their authority amidst unfamiliar surroundings (Kennedy, 2004). While maintaining order, they also introduced Islam and the Arabic language, setting in motion a slow, gradual process of cultural assimilation that irrevocably reshaped the social fabric of North Africa (Robinson, 2011).

North Africa's integration into the Islamic world was not a momentary act but an enduring transformation. These initial conquests ignited a ripple effect—one that would eventually propel Islamic influence into the Iberian Peninsula and beyond. The region, which had once been a fractured collection of Byzantine and tribal domains, became a linchpin of the Islamic empire. What began with rapid campaigns waged by determined armies across unforgiving landscapes evolved into a centuries-long legacy of cultural exchange, religious diffusion, and political influence. The dust of conquest settled, but the changes it wrought would resonate far beyond the deserts of North Africa, shaping the delicate balance of power across Europe and the Mediterranean.

The Spread into the Iberian Peninsula

The Islamic foray into the Iberian Peninsula was not merely an incursion; it was a defining wave that reshaped the tides of European history. A tumultuous saga of upheaval and transformation, it was catalysed in the early 8th century by an event both swift and spectacular. In 711, Tariq ibn Ziyad—leading a relatively small yet resolute force—crossed the narrow waters of the Strait of Gibraltar. On European soil, a highly unstable Visigothic kingdom, fractured by internal discord and failing leadership, lay ripe for conquest. The Muslim forces, capitalising on this disarray, executed an astonishingly rapid campaign, dismantling this crumbling dominion with remarkable ease.

However, conquest thrives not only on swords but also on circumstances. Among the oppressed folds of the Visigothic society—Hispano-Romans and Jewish communities in particular—discontent brewed. Years of harsh Visigothic rule had alienated these populations, fostering resentment that ultimately paved the way for the invaders. Some offered quiet acquiescence, while others extended more tangible support, a dynamic that accelerated the Muslim advance. By 718, the vast majority of the Iberian Peninsula was firmly in Islamic hands, save for the defiant, untamed pockets of resistance in the rugged northern highlands. Here, tenacious groups, isolated yet determined, planted the seeds of a long struggle to reclaim their lost lands.

Understanding the region's immense strategic value, the Umayyad Caliphate in Damascus moved swiftly to consolidate control. Governors were dispatched, tasked not only with the administration of new lands but with integrating the peninsula into the intricate web of the sprawling Islamic empire. Yet, military conquest was merely the overture to profound socio-political change. The Visigothic legal systems gave way to Islamic jurisprudence, establishing a fundamentally different mode of governance. Architectural wonders soon emerged, their grandeur commanding both respect and awe. Mosques, palaces, and defensive fortifications rose, silent yet eloquent declarations of Islamic permanence.

However, the transformation of the Iberian Peninsula went beyond structures of stone and mortar. Islamic culture began to intertwine with local traditions, creating a rich confluence of Islamic, Christian, and Jewish influences. From this cultural synthesis arose an exceptional epoch of intellectual and artistic brilliance, one that not only redefined the region but also emanated ripples of change throughout Europe. Far more than a mere military conquest, the Islamic rule of Iberia left an indelible mark, its legacy an enduring chapter of European civilisation's story.

The Emergence of the Umayyad Caliphate

The Umayyad Caliphate's ascendance was nothing short of monumental—a sprawling empire stretching across three continents that defined a new era for the Islamic world. Rooted in Damascus, this dynasty revolutionised the structures of governance, expanding its dominion while binding together a world of bewildering diversity. Nowhere was its imprint more profound than in the Iberian Peninsula, where the Umayyad administration not only consolidated power but also fostered a thriving, sophisticated society.

Incorporating the Iberian Peninsula into the caliphate's vast expanse presented challenges of governance, cultural adaptation, and administrative coherence. The Umayyads navigated these complexities by initiating comprehensive reforms, meticulously crafting systems designed to encourage growth and stability. Taxation and trade were restructured, creating pathways for economic integration. This era of meticulous administration did more than merely sustain the region—it allowed it to flourish. Under the Umayyads, Cordoba rose to unprecedented prominence. A city that once played a peripheral role became a dazzling epicentre of artistic innovation and intellectual fervour, rivalled by few across the medieval world.

Cordoba was not merely a city; it was a statement. Its bustling markets overflowed with goods imported from distant lands, a testament to the interconnected Islamic world. The grand mosque of Cordoba emerged as a crowning jewel, blending architectural audacity with spiritual magnificence. Meanwhile, the city's libraries and learning institutions amassed vast troves of knowledge, fostering a culture of scholarship that attracted the brightest minds of the era. Under the Umayyads, Córdoba became a quintessential beacon of cosmopolitanism, illuminating a unique civilisational brilliance that went far beyond conquest-driven dominance.

Yet the expansive reach of the caliphate concealed deep vulnerabilities. Internal divisions—fanned by tribal rivalries, political jockeying, and regional aspirations—began to gnaw at the foundations of unity. The very diversity that was initially an asset became, in moments of tension, a source of fragility. Governing territories so vast, with populations so varied in ethnicity, religion, and culture, proved an unwieldy task. External threats further compounded these difficulties, ensuring that the caliphate's supremacy was invariably contested.

Even so, the Umayyads' legacy endures far beyond their eventual decline. Islamic rule in the Iberian Peninsula fostered a mosaic of interwoven traditions, where Muslim, Christian, and Jewish influences braided into a tapestry of profound creativity and collaboration. This fertile exchange of ideas heralded a cultural and intellectual renaissance that resonated long after the Umayyads themselves faded from power. It was in their Iberian realm that a confluence of artistry, science, and philosophy brought forth a legacy whose reverberations shaped not only Spain but the broader currents of history itself.

In the shadow of conquest, in the glow of cultural radiance, the story of the Umayyads in al-Andalus remains one of history's most remarkable chapters—where swords delivered lands, but ideas delivered immortality.

Challenges Faced by Islamic Forces

The expansion of Islamic forces into Europe was fraught with formidable challenges that tested their military ingenuity, endurance, and adaptability. Chief among these hurdles was the daunting geography of the European landscape (Kennedy, 2004). Rugged mountain ranges like the Pyrenees and Alps, dense forests, and broad rivers such as the Rhône and Ebro created considerable logistical obstacles. Armies had to traverse these complex terrains, often under harsh conditions, pushing the boundaries of their strategic capabilities (Robinson, 2011). Beyond topography, resistance from local European forces was both fierce and persistent. Christian kingdoms such as the Visigoths in Hispania and the Franks in Gaul posed determined opposition, employing local knowledge and superior defensive fortifications to repulse invasions (Dickie, 2007). These adversaries were frequently well-equipped and united by a conviction to preserve their territories, making conquests arduous and costly (Holt, 2006).

Moreover, the unfamiliar climate of Europe introduced further complications. Extreme weather, from the biting cold of northern winters to the sweltering heat of southern summers, strained the physical and logistical capacities of Islamic armies, requiring significant adaptation to sustain campaigns (Gibb, 1969). Within their ranks, the Islamic forces also grappled with internal challenges. The cultural, linguistic, and ethnic diversity of their soldiers and allied factions often gave rise to tensions and miscommunications, sometimes threatening the cohesion of their expeditions (Seddon, 2012). Commanders had to walk a fine line, balancing the interests of disparate groups to maintain unity in purpose and discipline on the field.

Despite these obstacles, the Islamic forces displayed remarkable resilience and adaptability, devising innovative tactics and leveraging their expansive resource network to sustain their advances (Bennison, A.K. 2009). These qualities ultimately underpinned their ability to establish a lasting presence and deeply influence the regions they touched.

Alliance with Indigenous Groups

One of the Islamic forces' key strategies for overcoming resistance and solidifying control in newly conquered territories was forging alliances with indigenous groups. These alliances provided critical advantages, both militarily and politically, as they integrated local populations into the expanding Islamic domain (Fierro, M. 2005). By partnering with tribes and communities, the Islamic forces gained invaluable intelligence about the local terrain, supply routes, and hidden dangers. Such insider knowledge allowed them to navigate unfamiliar regions and avoid unnecessary losses (Hourani, A. 2010).

Beyond strategic insights, local allies frequently augmented the Islamic forces' logistical capacity. Tribes contributed shelter, provisions, and manpower, enabling armies to maintain supply lines critical for their operations (McCormick, 2001). In some cases, indigenous groups even served as auxiliary forces, bolstering the Islamic armies and cementing shared interests (Robinson, 2011). These partnerships also facilitated smoother transitions of power. By including local elites in governance structures or offering favourable terms to indigenous leaders, Islamic rulers fostered cooperation and reduced resistance to their authority.

Importantly, alliances were often symbiotic. Indigenous factions stood to benefit from Islamic rule through new trade opportunities, access to advanced knowledge, and protection against rival tribes or oppressive rulers (Glick, 1999). This mutual dependency strengthened bonds between conquering and local forces, creating a climate of collaboration that extended beyond military conquests. Ultimately, the ability to work with local populations played a decisive role in the Islamic forces' success, not only in terms of territorial expansion but also in embedding their influence across diverse communities.

Impact on European Societies

The Islamic conquests left an indelible mark on European societies, triggering profound transformations across cultural, social, and economic dimensions. Perhaps most striking was the introduction of Islamic scientific and intellectual advancements. Through translations, the works of Islamic scholars passed into Europe, reinvigorating fields such as astronomy, mathematics, medicine, and philosophy (Bennison, A.K. 2009). This diffusion of knowledge helped lay the foundations for the European Renaissance, highlighting the vital role of Islamic contributions to Europe's intellectual awakening.

Aesthetic and artistic exchanges also flourished. The intricate geometric patterns, arabesques, and architectural styles of Islamic art profoundly influenced European artisans and builders, inspiring designs that bridged cultural boundaries (Glick, 1999). This exchange birthed unique artistic movements, such as the Mudejar style in Spain, blending Islamic and European elements into harmonious forms (Lambton, 1988). These cultural integrations enriched local traditions and underscored the enduring legacy of Islamic influence on European creativity.

Economically, the Islamic conquests fostered the development of extensive trade networks, connecting Europe to the thriving centres of the Islamic world in the Middle East and North Africa (Esposito, 2016). Luxuries such as spices, silk, and glass flowed through European markets, while innovations in irrigation, crop rotations, and agronomy revolutionised agriculture (Brett & Fentress, 1996). These advancements increased productivity, reshaped rural economies, and catalysed urban growth, bringing prosperity to regions once on the periphery of global trade (Ibn Khaldun, 1990).

Demographically, the Islamic conquests also cultivated diversity in European societies. Muslim populations settled in conquered territories, notably in Al-Andalus, where the coexistence of Muslim, Christian, and Jewish communities created a pluralistic society characterised by collaboration and tolerance (Robinson, 2011). This multicultural coexistence fostered a fertile ground for intellectual and cultural exchange, where European, Islamic, and Jewish traditions collectively thrived (Glick, 1999). The resulting synthesis enriched European societies, creating a legacy of innovation, trade, and cultural vibrancy.

In sum, the Islamic expansion into Europe was not merely a tale of military conquests but a transformative era that reshaped Europe's historical trajectory. Its impacts ripple through history, reflecting the interconnectedness of these once-diverse worlds (Esposito, 2016).

Cultural and Intellectual Exchange

The Islamic conquests of Europe ignited one of history's most profound cultural and intellectual crossroads, where the boundaries of civilisations blurred in an extraordinary torrent of ideas, innovations, and artistic vibrancy (Brett & Fentress, 1996). What unfolded was not merely a conquest of territories but a conquest of minds—a sudden flourishing of knowledge transfer that would alter the destiny of continents (Bennison, A.K. 2009). Islamic scholars, consumed by a keen intellectual curiosity, stood as the linchpins of this cultural symbiosis, safeguarding the wisdom of antiquity. They ardently translated Greek classics—from the piercing logic of Aristotle to the metaphysical musings of Plato—imbuing Europe's dormant scholasticism with new life during the so-called "Dark Ages" and sowing seeds for the Renaissance centuries later (Glick, 1999; Esposito, 2016).

However, this transfer of legacy did not rest on philosophy alone. Mathematics leapt forward as Arabic numerals, born in the East, supplanted cumbersome Roman systems, bringing with them the zero—an enigma that would revolutionise calculation and the sciences (Hourani, A. 2010). Medicine, illuminated by Islamic innovation, shifted paradigms in surgery and pharmacology. Astronomy, too, found its stars realigned, with Islamic contributions charting new celestial paths for European advancements.

This effusion of knowledge spilt into tangible aesthetics—architecture and art transformed under the spell of Islamic geometric design, with its symmetrical intricacies weaving into the very fabric of Europe's cathedrals and manuscripts (Collins, R. 2014). Beyond the high arts lay the softer, more intangible consequences of this exchange: the mutual weaving of customs, cuisines, and traditions that lent credence to coexistence and lent Europe an undeniable multicultural substratum (Ibn Khaldun, 1990). The process, while uneven, generated a hybrid vigour, a dynamic interplay of influences that reshaped Europe into a cultural palimpsest. In this, the Islamic conquests did not merely bridge two civilisations—they spun an enduring web of shared human endeavour, delicately threading the past to the future (Esposito, 1998).

Role of Religion in Conquests

Religion—gravely celestial yet profoundly terrestrial—course through the veins of the Islamic conquests of Europe, not so much as a mere tool but as a defining heartbeat. Amid the dust of battle and whispers of diplomacy, the banners of Islam bore not just political ambitions but divine decree, making faith both sword and solace (Fierro, M. 2005). The concept of *jihad*, enshrined in Islamic doctrine emerged as both a rallying cry and a moral justification, imbuing warriors with fervour and legitimising expansion as a spiritual duty (Esposito, 2016).

Yet, this divine mandate met an already bristling tapestry of Christian Europe. Here, religion forged the frontlines as much as the sword itself, with Christianity and Islam clashing not merely as political rivals but as parallel cosmos of belief (Holt, 2006). For the conquered peoples, these clashes produced a spectrum of experiences—ranging from subjugation and resistance to uneasy coexistence. While Islamic rulers often extended protected status to Christian and Jewish "People of the Book" through *dhimmi* policies, the realities of discriminatory taxation and social stratification could incite friction (Seddon, 2012). Meanwhile, for Muslim converts, religion also promised liberation from such hierarchies, compounding Islam's political magnetism with spiritual allure.

This interplay of faiths transcended battlefields and dominions: religious institutes emerged as beacons of learning, their libraries brimming with manuscripts that fused Islamic scholarship with local heritages (Ibn Khaldun, 1990). From mysticism to metaphysics, divine perspectives blended—a mosaic at once contentious and coalescent, filled with ambivalences. In truth, religion shaped these conquests less as a monolithic, overarching force and more as an intricate, dual-edged instrument—both a rationale for divisions and a bridge that shifted Europe toward interfaith cultural dynamism (McCormick, 2001). Faith, therefore, was not simply chronicled in these conquests as a creed—it became an abiding lens through which power, identity, and exchange were conceived.

Evaluating Legacy and Historical Perspectives

To grasp the legacy of the Islamic conquests of Europe is to sift through layers of contested narratives—some engrained, others shifting beneath the force of modern scholarship (Holt, 2006). Traditionally painted as violent subversion—an "us" versus "them" binary—the stories of these conquests often echo the larger anxieties of identity and belonging, and scholars have found it necessary to dismantle such simplifications (Seddon, 2012). Indeed, the historical legacy reveals not blunt tyranny but the nuanced interplay between exogenous forces and local adaptation.

Islamic governance left an indelible imprint on the regions it touched, constructing novel administrative systems while adapting to and reshaping the local customs they encountered. From judicial reforms to tax systems, Islamic rule subtly reoriented the local axis of civic and legal structures while often coexisting with older frameworks, creating a multifaceted governance model (Fierro, M. 2005). In regions such as Al-Andalus, syncretism blossomed, where Moorish governance intertwined with Iberian cultural streams, forming a generation of artistic and philosophical zeniths unparalleled in Europe (Glick, 1999).

The intellectual legacy alone laid Europe's future into unanticipated trajectories. The reintroduction and reinterpretation of classical antiquity—and Islam's enhancements to it—reshaped the ethos of European learning and injected vitality into fields such as science and architecture (Esposito, 2016). And yet, these legacies are not without ambivalence; the Islamic advancements in Europe sometimes came at the expense of displacement, marginalisation, or coercion. Thus, to evaluate the conquests' legacy is to wrestle with contradictions—the violence that accompanied prosperity, the subjugation that seeded progress, and the division that paradoxically cultivated interconnectedness (Robinson, 2011).

What persists most enduringly, perhaps, is not the wars that were fought but the worlds that were shaped. Today's scholarship seeks to transcend outdated polemics of civilisational clashes, focusing instead on the dynamism of exchange and hybridity (Bennison, A.K. 2009). For what the Islamic conquests left Europe was not just kingdoms redrawn but paradigms reordered—a reawakening, through conflict and collaboration, of a shared heritage. The unfolding narrative is no longer one of mere Muslim conquerors or European victims but of a tapestry that weaves both as reciprocal architects of a more complex and enriched human story.

Chapter 3

Overview of Key Questions and Puzzles

The Context of the Islamic Conquests in Europe

The Islamic conquests in Europe stand as a seminal chapter in the continent's history, profoundly altering its political, cultural, and religious fabric. Beginning in the 7th century, Islamic forces undertook expansive campaigns, leveraging a convergence of motivations—religious zeal, political ambition, and economic objectives (Hawting, 2000; Crone, 2003). Europe at the time was a fragmented landscape, teeming with rival kingdoms and empires endlessly vying for dominion. This division proved to be fertile ground for the advancing Islamic armies, who skillfully exploited the disunity to extend their influence and territorial holdings (Hodgson, 1974).

The rapid rise of Islam in the Middle East and North Africa set the stage for its expansion into Europe (Lapidus, 1988). To

Islamic rulers, Europe appeared as a land of untapped opportunities—strategically vital, resource-rich, and ripe for conquest. Yet, these campaigns were not purely about territorial gain; they were deeply infused with a sense of divine mission—the expansion of Islamic rule seen as a means of spreading a faith they believed was destined to illuminate the world (Menocal, 2002). Through their own lens, Islamic conquerors viewed themselves as agents of civilisation, bringers of enlightenment to the so-called barbarous lands of Europe (Rosenthal, 1975).

Military ingenuity and political cunning characterised these campaigns (Kennedy, 1996). Islamic forces employed advanced tactics—masterful use of cavalry, innovative siege warfare, and even psychological strategies to unsettle their foes (Ibn Khaldun, 1967). Diplomacy, too, played a crucial role, as Islamic leaders forged alliances with opportunistic local rulers and manipulated internal discord to further their goals (Gibb, 1963).

While conquest often meant conflict, the Islamic approach was not universally aggressive. In certain cases, conquest came via negotiation or cultural assimilation rather than outright warfare. To ensure a smoother integration, Islamic rulers would frequently permit local customs and traditions to persist under the overarching framework of their rule (Collins, 1989). Such strategies not only mitigated local resistance but also fostered an atmosphere of cooperation between conquerors and conquerors.

Ultimately, the Islamic conquests in Europe were transformative. They ushered in significant cultural exchanges, heightened trade networks, and planted the seeds for intellectual growth on both sides of the Mediterranean (Blair, 2000). The ripples of these events still resonate in contemporary Europe, shaping its historical identity and geopolitical developments (Tolan, 2013).

The Motivations of Islamic Conquerors

The motivations driving the medieval Islamic conquerors in their European campaigns were as varied as they were intricate. Central to their efforts was a profound religious conviction—a determination to spread Islam's teachings and expand the rule of the Caliphate into new lands (Hodgson, 1974). Conquest, in this sense, was more than material ambition; it was seen as a sacred act of fulfilling a divine mandate to bring non-Muslim territories under Islamic governance (Menocal, 2002).

Yet religion alone does not paint the full picture. Political and economic aspirations fuelled the campaigns with equal intensity. Conquering fertile lands and resource-rich regions was a way to bolster the wealth and power of the Islamic state (Rosenthal, 1975). These newly acquired territories strengthened the Caliphate's geopolitical standing, consolidating authority over rivals and projecting its dominance across a widening expanse (Lapidus, 1988).

Beyond the practicalities of faith and politics lay the human craving for glory and renown. For Islamic conquerors, military success brought unparalleled prestige, elevating leaders and soldiers alike within their societies and securing their legacies for posterity (Kennedy, 1996). The allure of fame was often accompanied by the spirit of adventure—a drive to traverse unknown lands, confront new challenges, and engrain their names in the historical tapestry of their culture (Crone, 2003).

Thus, the motives of Islamic conquerors defy simplistic categorisation, revealing a spectrum of intertwined factors—spiritual, political, economic, and personal—that propelled them into the heart of Europe's tumultuous medieval landscape (Hawting, 2000).

The Resistance Faced by Islamic Forces

The Islamic advances into Europe encountered fierce resistance, shaped by the diverse cultural, political, and religious makeup of the territories they sought to dominate. Local rulers, often deeply embedded in their own traditions, resolutely defended their homelands, deploying everything from well-coordinated armies to guerrilla tactics. The landscape itself, with its rugged mountains, dense forests, and unforgiving weather, presented its own share of challenges, slowing the advancing Islamic forces and testing their resolve (Ibn Khaldun, 1967).

A defining moment in this resistance came during the Battle of Tours in 732. Here, the Frankish forces, under the leadership of Charles Martel, decisively repelled Islamic armies, halting their further advance into the heart of what is now France (Hawting, 2000). The Franks, equipped with superior cavalry and deft military strategies, stood as a powerful bulwark. Their triumph was not just a matter of military strength but also of unity, underpinned by a shared cultural and religious identity that galvanised their cause (Tolan, 2013).

Resistance was not always confined to the battlefield. Diplomacy and strategic alliances also served as tools against Islamic expansion. The Byzantine Empire, for instance, mounted a stiff defence using its fortified cities, naval superiority, and formidable strategic acumen (Lapidus, 1988). Fortified by their deeply entrenched Christian faith and a strong sense of cultural distinctiveness, the Byzantines presented an enduring challenge to the advancing Islamic forces (Blair, 2000).

In many instances, it was not solely about military might or strategy. Cultural and religious distinctions often inflamed opposition, with local populations perceiving Islamic conquerors as outsiders seeking to impose an alien way of life. These ideological divisions were as much a battleground as the fields of conflict themselves, intensifying the fervour with which local populations resisted (Rosenthal, 1975; Menocal, 2002).

The resistance endured by Islamic forces demanded adaptability. They adjusted their strategies, often combining military might with psychological and diplomatic tactics. This interplay of confrontation, negotiation, and cultural exchange demonstrated not only the resolve of the defenders but also the resilience and ingenuity of the Islamic conquerors. These clashes, shaped by competing faiths, values, and ambitions, ultimately forged the complex dynamics of the medieval world (Hodgson, 1974).

The Role of Religion in the Conquests

Religion served as an essential catalyst in the Islamic conquests of Europe, shaping their motivations, scope, and execution. The Muslim expansion was not solely a territorial or militaristic endeavour—it was profoundly tied to a religious mission aimed at propagating Islam in lands perceived as unlit by its truths (Crone, 2003). Conquerors often framed their efforts as fulfilling a divine mandate to spread the faith. The doctrine of jihad—understood in this context as a spiritual and material struggle—became the theological foundation for military campaigns, backed by both religious leaders and Islamic doctrine (Ibn Khaldun, 1967).

The promise of celestial rewards animated many fighters, who saw these campaigns as not only a duty but a path to eternal salvation (Tolan, 2013). Such fervour strengthened their resolve in battles and inspired remarkable unity amidst military challenges. Yet religion was not solely about conquest itself; it also fundamentally influenced the relationships between Muslim invaders and local populations. While some embraced Islam voluntarily, viewing it as liberating or advantageous, others resisted conversions, leading to unavoidable social frictions (Blair, 2000). In many cases, conquered territories were governed under Sharia law, with the introduction of Islamic customs reconfiguring societal norms and practices (Hawting, 2000).

Beyond the immediate period of conquest, religion's role extended into the creation of long-term cultural legacies. Islamic beliefs and practices gradually permeated the cultural and political frameworks of certain European regions, leaving an indelible mark on local governance and artistic expression (Rosenthal, 1975). The resulting confluence of Islamic and European traditions enriched the cultural fabric, birthing unique architectural styles, literary forms, and philosophical discourse (Gibb, 1963).

Thus, religion functioned not merely as a motivating force but also as an enduring thread interweaving the trajectory of these conquests and their later consequences. Its influence was palpable in the zeal of the warriors, the integration of societal norms, and the profound changes it wrought upon European life and history.

The Impact on European Societies

The Islamic conquests triggered profound and far-reaching transformations within Europe, reshaping its political, economic, social, and cultural dimensions. The political map of Europe evolved under the shadow of the conquerors as Islamic rule advanced into regions like the Iberian Peninsula, challenging existing state boundaries and reshuffling power dynamics (Hodgson, 1974). Muslim rulers established highly organised administrative systems, setting local precedence for governance that included meritocratic bureaucracy and legal uniformity.

Perhaps one of the most enduring impacts of the conquests was the cross-pollination of ideas and technologies. Islamic achievements in science, medicine, and mathematics flowed into Europe, catalysing intellectual and practical innovation (Blair, 2000). The translation of scientific and philosophical texts from Arabic into Latin ensured that knowledge preserved and expanded in the Islamic world significantly informed European progress. This intellectual exchange was instrumental in the later Renaissance (Lapidus, 1988).

Economically, the conquests integrated Europe into a broader transcontinental trade network, increasing overall prosperity. The introduction of Islamic fiscal systems and practices, such as checks (sakk) and credit instruments, revolutionised economic affairs, while trade routes established by Islamic rulers enabled the movement of goods, wealth, and ideas (Rosenthal, 1975). Such innovations fundamentally altered the economic structures of European societies, linking them more closely with the vast Byzantine, North African, and Middle Eastern markets.

Socially and culturally, the impact of the Islamic conquests was both transformative and syncretic. Islamic styles of art, architecture, and literature flourished in territories under Muslim rule, with timeless examples like the Alhambra in Spain epitomising this fusion (Gibb, 1963). The coexistence of Muslim, Christian, and Jewish communities within certain territories, particularly in al-Andalus, cultivated a degree of multiculturalism rare for the era. However, this coexistence was not without its conflicts and moments of intolerance.

The exchanges that took place during and after the Islamic conquests also affected religious life in profound ways. The theological dialogues and encounters between Muslims, Christians, and Jews enriched all three religious traditions while introducing Islamic practices and cosmologies to broader European spiritual contexts (Tolan, 2013). Yet these interactions also planted seeds of friction that would manifest later during periods like the Crusades.

Ultimately, the Islamic conquests redefined Europe's place within the Mediterranean world, sparking changes whose aftershocks are visible centuries later. The economic, cultural, and social interweaving fostered by these conquests helped create the complex mosaic that is modern Europe.

The Legacy of the Conquests

The legacy of the Islamic conquests in Europe endures and continues to shape historical and cultural memory. Among their most immediate and visible impacts was the centuries-long integration and cultural synthesis that occurred between Islamic and European civilisations. This mingling brought forth unparalleled knowledge exchange during periods like the Golden Age of Islam, with Muslim scholars acting as intermediaries who preserved, expanded, and disseminated the scientific and philosophical achievements of antiquity (Tolan, 2013). The preservation and eventual reintroduction of works by philosophers such as Aristotle and Euclid directly influenced the intellectual trajectory of medieval Europe and its subsequent Renaissance (Rosenthal, 1975).

The cultural impacts extended to the aesthetic and architectural arena. Islamic architectural influences flourished, as evidenced in iconic structures like the Great Mosque of Córdoba and the Giralda Tower in Seville. The blending of local European styles with Islamic designs gave rise to forms that remain celebrated today (Blair, 2000). In art, the use of intricate geometric patterns, calligraphy, and arabesques inspired new approaches to composition and form within European artistic traditions (Hodgson, 1974).

The culinary and linguistic spheres also bear marks of this legacy. Arabic words became embedded within European vocabularies, influencing fields ranging from science to daily life. Additionally, the use of spices, irrigation techniques, and culinary traditions introduced by Muslim societies altered European cuisines in ways still evident today (Menocal, 2002).

Religiously, the legacy of coexistence and interaction in regions such as al-Andalus illustrates both the highs and lows of interfaith exchange. While moments of cooperation brought periods of remarkable tolerance and cultural flourishing, the eventual Christian Reconquista and associated expulsions also revealed the fragile complexities of these relationships (Lapidus, 1988).

Economically, the trade networks forged between Islamic and European states helped to lay the foundations for later mercantile and colonial expansions. The interconnected Mediterranean world facilitated by the Islamic conquests proved instrumental in the rise of European economic power and global exploration (Gibb, 1963).

Ultimately, the legacy of the Islamic conquests in Europe is a dual narrative: one of conflict and conquest, but also one of exchange, integration, and mutual enrichment. These conquests altered the trajectory not only of Europe but also of global history, and their lasting imprint continues to provoke debate and inspire study to this day (Collins, 1989).

Unanswered Questions and Historical Debates

The history of the Islamic conquests in Europe presents a web of unresolved questions and contentious debates that have shaped scholarly discourse for decades. Foremost among these debates is the lasting impact of these conquests on European societies. On one side, some historians argue that the influence was profound, significantly shaping Europe's cultural, scientific, and architectural development. They point to elements such as the introduction of advanced scientific knowledge, architectural styles seen in structures like the Great Mosque of Córdoba, and linguistic borrowings (e.g., Arabic-derived terms in Spanish) as evidence of this profound impact. Ibn Khaldun (1967), for instance, posits that the Islamic presence served as a cultural and intellectual bridge between the classical and medieval worlds, catalysing advancements in European learning.

Contrastingly, other scholars contend that the effects were relatively superficial, with Islamic rule failing to penetrate deeply enough to alter the core fabric of Christian European societies significantly. Bernard Lewis and others argue that once Islamic rule receded, many regions reverted to earlier traditions with minimal lasting influence (Lapidus, 1988). This duality raises the question: were the Islamic conquests a fleeting episode in European history or a transformative period with enduring legacies?

The motives behind the conquests also remain under scrutiny. While the narrative of religious zeal as a driving force is often highlighted, particularly through the concept of jihad, other historians emphasise political and economic motivations. The quest for territorial expansion, the acquisition of wealth through plunder and trade routes, and power consolidation are often viewed as practical factors undergirding the conquests. Alvarez (2012) argues for an interplay of both religious and economic motives, showing how religion provided a unifying framework for what were often pragmatic ambitions. This dual interpretation raises deeper questions about the role of religion during expansions: Was Islam primarily the justification for conquest, or did it act as a deeply ingrained motive influencing actions and governance?

Another contentious point concerns the nature of local resistance. Primary accounts and modern interpretations diverge when assessing the extent to which Islamic forces met resistance or encountered willing collaborators. Gibb (1963) portrays resistance as fierce and widespread, pointing to battles like the

Battle of Covadonga (718) in northern Spain as instances where locals resisted conquest and later catalysed the Christian Reconquista. Conversely, Hodgson (1974) discusses instances of integration and collaboration between Islamic rulers and local elites, either through alliances or pragmatism to maintain power. This duality invites further exploration of individual regions: Did different areas experience conquest as a cataclysmic upheaval or a gradual process of accommodation?

These unanswered questions about the societal impact, motivations for conquest, and varying local responses highlight the nuanced and complex nature of the Islamic conquests in Europe. They also underscore the necessity of further research to uncover the deeper truths of this historical period.

Key Figures and Leaders in the Conquests

The pivotal figures of the Islamic conquests in Europe were not only architects of military triumphs but also shapers of enduring legacies that rippled through history. Each leader contributed distinctively, influencing the trajectory of conquests and the societies they encompassed.

Tariq ibn Ziyad is perhaps the most notable figure in the narrative of the Islamic expansion into Europe. In 711 CE, as the leader of a Berber-Arab force, he spearheaded the invasion of the Iberian Peninsula, landing in Gibraltar (a name derived from *Jabal Tariq*, or "Mount of Tariq"). His decisive victory at the Battle of Guadalete or Wadi Lakka against the Visigothic King Roderic marked a turning point, enabling the rapid expansion of Islamic rule in Spain. Tariq's strategic acuity and charismatic leadership cemented his place in history as a transformative figure (Gibb, 1963).

The consolidation of Islamic control and cultural flourishing in Spain owed much to Abd al-Rahman I, the founder of the Umayyad Emirate of Córdoba. Fleeing the Abbasid persecution of the Umayyads in the Middle East, Abd al-Rahman sought refuge in Spain in 756 CE. There, he established an independent emirate, organising a stable administration and fostering a cultural renaissance. Abd al-Rahman's reign transformed Córdoba into a centre of learning, architectural innovation, and interfaith interaction, laying the groundwork for the so-called Golden Age of Al-Andalus. His diplomacy and resilience ensured the survival of Umayyad authority in Europe amidst internal and external pressures (Menocal, 2002).

Turning toward the east, Khalid ibn al-Walid, while more prominently remembered for campaigns in the Middle East and the Byzantine front, also impacted regions bordering Europe, including the Balkans and southern territories of the Byzantine Empire. Renowned as *Saif Allah* (the Sword of God), Khalid's military genius was exemplified through his ability to adapt to diverse theatres of war. His campaigns opened pathways for Islamic influence in Europe, reflecting the wider strategic ambitions of early Islamic powers (Ibn Khaldun, 1967; Lapidus, 1988).

In a more stabilising role, the Abbasid Caliph Harun al-Rashid emerges as a key player in consolidating Islamic rule and fostering diplomacy between the Islamic world and Europe. Harun, whose reign coincided with Charlemagne's in Western Europe, navigated these complex relationships with tact, engaging in exchanges of envoys and gifts that hinted at mutual respect and rivalry. While not directly linked to conquests, his governance helped sustain the political frameworks that emerged from earlier campaigns (Hodgson, 1974).

These leaders exemplify the diversity of approaches—military, political, cultural, and diplomatic—that defined European Islamic conquests. From ambitious generals like Tariq ibn Ziyad to visionary statesmen like Abd al-Rahman I and Harun al-Rashid, their contributions offer a multifaceted understanding of the conquests and their enduring legacies in history.

Comparisons with Other Conquests in History

When comparing the Islamic conquests in Europe to other large-scale historical conquests, one finds both striking similarities and important distinctions. Central to these comparisons are the methods employed by the conquering forces, the lasting effects on the conquered regions, and the charisma and leadership of key figures.

The **military and social strategies** utilised in the Islamic conquests bear some resemblance to those of earlier empires like the Roman and Mongol Empires but remain uniquely nuanced. The Roman Empire's expansion, for instance, involved the systematic integration of conquered peoples into its political and administrative framework as a tool for maintaining stability across its vast holdings. Similarly, the Islamic conquerors combined **military innovation and political diplomacy**, often accommodating local leaders, cultures, and practices in exchange for loyalty or the adoption of Islamic governance.

THE ISLAMIC CONQUESTS IN EUROPE ~ 51

Examples of this strategic flexibility can be seen in the treaties struck during the early conquests of Al-Andalus.

Comparatively, the **Mongol conquests** employed far more brutal tactics, relying on fear and mass destruction to subdue resistance. Yet both the Islamic and Mongol campaigns involved a **fusion of cultures and the establishment of thriving trade networks**. The Mongols ushered in a period of unprecedented cross-continental exchange along the Silk Road, while the Islamic conquests strengthened economic connections between Europe, the Middle East, and North Africa, solidifying their role as intermediaries of trade and knowledge.

In terms of impact, **long-term cultural and societal transformations** are hallmarks of history's great conquests, including this one. Just as Roman governance systems influenced European legal and political traditions for centuries, the Islamic conquests introduced **scientific, philosophical, and cultural advancements** to European societies—most notably in Spain. The transfer of knowledge in fields like medicine, astronomy, and mathematics had a profound ripple effect during the medieval period and shaped the intellectual groundwork for later movements, such as the European Renaissance.

Turning to the **key figures in these conquests**, parallels emerge. Leaders like Tariq ibn Ziyad and Abd al-Rahman I during the Islamic campaigns shared common traits with figures such as Alexander the Great, who conceptualised unified dominions through clever alliance-building and battlefield resolution. Similarly, Genghis Khan's decisive command and the Mongols' remarkable mobility echoed the adaptation and resourcefulness seen in the Islamic forces of the 7th and 8th centuries. Yet, while Genghis Khan and Alexander often sought secular glory and worldly dominion, the Islamic conquerors were frequently motivated by a **religious dimension**, pursuing the establishment of a polity governed by Islamic principles, which fundamentally shaped the cultural identities of the conquered territories.

It's also important to note the **distinctive role of religion** in the Islamic conquests compared to its historical counterparts. While many empires justified expansion through divine right or political necessity, the Islamic conquests entwined military success with the spread of religious doctrine. This dual function of conquest as both **spiritual and territorial expansion** is a defining feature that differentiates the Islamic campaigns from the purely secular ambitions of empires like Rome or the Mongols.

In sum, the Islamic conquests in Europe stand as both a mirror to and a divergence from other landmark conquests in history. While they share elements of military execution, cultural exchanges, and enduring influence with the likes of the Romans and Mongols, they are distinguished by their fusion of **religious mission, political pragmatism, and cultural synthesis**, leaving a uniquely lasting legacy.

Future Implications of the Islamic Conquests in Europe

The Islamic conquests in Europe continue to hold significant implications for contemporary and future discussions about cultural interaction, historical interpretation, and societal development. They provide a critical lens through which to view and understand the dynamic relationships between Islam and Europe, both historically and in the modern era.

One major implication lies in the realm of **intercultural and interfaith dialogue**. European societies today, grappling with issues of multiculturalism and integration, can draw lessons from the historical coexistence of Islamic and Christian communities during periods such as **Medieval Spain** under Islamic rule. Concepts such as *convivencia* (coexistence) offer valuable insights into how diverse populations can thrive together through shared knowledge, economic exchange, and mutual respect for differences. By revisiting these historical moments, Europe can harness its past to promote **tolerance and unity** in navigating its multicultural present and future.

In the broader context of **global relations**, the understanding of Islamic contributions to European history has the potential to reshape narratives and foster a greater sense of connection between European and Muslim-majority nations. During the Islamic conquests, pioneering advances in science, art, philosophy, and trade flowed through Europe due to contact with the Islamic world. The enduring impact of these contributions is a reminder of the **interdependence of civilisations**. In today's realm of interconnected global economies, reflecting on this shared history could enhance collaboration across divides.

Another key implication lies in recognising the **economic and scientific foundations** laid during the Islamic conquests. The global trade routes established or solidified during the period have evolved into modern trading networks, and the knowledge disseminated during this era still underpins significant advancements in fields like engineering, architecture, and medicine. An acknowledgement of this legacy not only honours past achievements but also provides opportunities to forge closer ties in areas like **educational exchange and economic development**.

Lastly, the **symbolic weight of the conquests** influences modern debates about identity, belonging, and historical justice. For some, they serve as a point of pride, showcasing a period in which Islamic civilisation contributed meaningfully to global progress. For others, they remain a controversial chapter of history due to the violent nature of conquest. Striking a balanced interpretation of these events is crucial for fostering constructive dialogue about a shared past.

Looking outward, the history of the Islamic conquests can serve as a framework for addressing future challenges. Recognising the intricate histories of cultural overlap between Islamic and European societies can help break down stereotypes, encourage cross-cultural understanding, and create **a more inclusive narrative of global history**.

In conclusion, the Islamic conquests in Europe are more than just a historical event—they are **a living legacy** with tangible implications for the present and the future. By engaging thoughtfully with this past, Europe can continue to build bridges with its diverse populations, strengthen its ties with the Muslim world, and create a vision for a just, inclusive, and interconnected future.

Chapter 4

The Conquest of Spain

The Early Muslim Invasions: the initial incursions into the Iberian Peninsula by Muslim forces

The early Muslim invasions of the Iberian Peninsula were marked by a series of strategic incursions that laid the foundation for the eventual conquest of Visigothic Spain (Tolan, 2013). In the early 8th century, Muslim forces under the command of Tariq ibn Ziyad crossed the Strait of Gibraltar and landed on the shores of southern Spain (Gibb, 1963). These initial invasions were part of the broader Islamic expansion into Europe and aimed to establish a foothold in the region.

The Muslim armies, composed of Berber and Arab fighters, faced little resistance initially as they advanced inland, capturing cities and territories along the way (Hawting, 2000). The Visigothic Kingdom, weakened by internal strife and external threats, struggled to mount a cohesive defence against the invading forces (Lapidus, 1988). The speed and ferocity of the Muslim advance caught many by surprise, and soon, key strongholds fell to the advancing armies.

One of the pivotal moments in the early Muslim invasions was the Battle of Guadalete, a decisive conflict that would shape the course of Iberian history (Crone, 2003). Led by Tariq ibn Ziyad, the Muslim forces clashed with the Visigothic army near the Guadalete River. The battle was fierce, and despite being outnumbered, the Muslims achieved a resounding victory (Menocal, 2002). The fall of the Visigothic king, Roderic, marked the end of Visigothic rule in Spain and paved the way for Muslim dominance in the region.

The successful incursions into the Iberian Peninsula marked the beginning of a new era of Islamic rule in Spain, characterised by cultural exchange, scientific advancement, and religious tolerance (Tolan, 2013). The early Muslim invasions played a crucial role in shaping the destiny of the Iberian Peninsula and laid the foundation for the establishment of Al-Andalus, a dazzling civilisation that would flourish for centuries to come.

The Battle of Guadalete: the significant battle that led to the Muslim conquest of Visigothic Spain

The Battle of Guadalete in 711 CE marked a significant turning point in the history of the Iberian Peninsula (Gibb, 1963; Fletcher, Richard, 2006). Led by the Berber general Tariq ibn Ziyad, the Muslim forces clashed with the Visigothic army led by King Roderic. The exact location of the battle is still debated among historians, with some placing it near the Guadalete River in southern Spain.

Rumours of internal strife within the Visigothic kingdom provided an opportunity for Tariq to launch his campaign into Iberia (Hawting, 2000). With a relatively small force of around 7,000 soldiers, Tariq faced the larger Visigothic army, estimated to be over 20,000 strong (Lapidus, 1988). Despite being outnumbered, the Muslim troops, including Berbers and Syrian tribesmen, displayed remarkable discipline and tactics on the battlefield (Crone, 2003).

The battle was fierce and intense, lasting for several days. The Muslim cavalry, known for their swift and agile manoeuvres, played a crucial role in breaking through the Visigothic lines (Menocal, 2002). King Roderic himself was killed in the fighting, leading to the collapse of Visigothic resistance. The defeat at Guadalete marked the decisive victory that paved the way for the Muslim conquest of Visigothic Spain.

Following the battle, Tariq and his troops continued to advance, capturing key cities such as Toledo and Cordoba (Tolan, 2013). The fall of the Visigothic kingdom and the establishment of Muslim rule in Spain laid the foundation for the Umayyad Caliphate's dominance in the region. The Battle of Guadalete not only altered the political landscape of Iberia but also ushered in a new era of cultural exchange and coexistence between Muslims, Christians, and Jews in al-Andalus.

The establishment of the Umayyad Caliphate in Al-Andalus and the subsequent Islamic Golden Age were pivotal in shaping the cultural, political, and intellectual legacy of the Iberian Peninsula. Here's an in-depth overview of these transformative periods:

The Establishment of the Umayyad Caliphate in Spain

The Muslim conquest of the Iberian Peninsula began in 711 CE, catalysed by the decisive victory at the *Battle of Guadalete*. This battle marked the collapse of the Visigothic Kingdom, led by King Roderic, and opened the path for Muslim forces under commanders Tariq ibn Ziyad and Musa ibn Nusayr to advance rapidly across the region. Within a few years, much of the Iberian Peninsula, later known as *Al-Andalus*, fell under Muslim control.

However, the consolidation of Muslim rule was not solidified until a significant political restructuring occurred under the leadership of *Abd al-Rahman I*. Following the Abbasid revolution (750 CE), which overthrew the Umayyad dynasty in the Islamic heartlands, Abd al-Rahman I, a surviving Umayyad prince, fled to the Iberian Peninsula. In 756 CE, he established his authority over Al-Andalus, declaring himself *Amir* (ruler) and breaking political ties with the Abbasid Caliphate based in Baghdad. Abd al-Rahman I successfully reunited the fragmented Muslim factions in the region, stabilised his rule, and founded what would become the *Umayyad Emirate of Cordoba*.

To consolidate power, the Umayyads introduced a system of governance that amalgamated *Islamic principles with local customs and traditions*. A centralised administration was created, governed by appointees who effectively managed resources, upheld law and order, and ensured tax collection. Cities like Cordoba, Seville, and Toledo emerged as major centres of administration and commerce.

A key strategy employed by the Umayyads was the promotion and patronage of *Islamic culture and values*. They built grand mosques and palaces to symbolise their wealth and power, most notably the *Great Mosque of Cordoba*, which became a hallmark of Islamic architecture. This cultural emphasis established Al-Andalus as a beacon of Islamic civilisation, attracting scholars, artisans, and individuals seeking prosperity.

Consolidation and the Foundations of Al-Andalus' Prosperity

Under Abd al-Rahman I and his successors, Al-Andalus transitioned from an emirate to a thriving centre of Islamic governance. This process culminated in 929 CE when Abd al-Rahman III declared himself *Caliph*, elevating Cordoba to the status of a supreme political and cultural capital. The *Umayyad Caliphate of Cordoba* (929–1031 CE) saw the Iberian Peninsula reach unprecedented heights of prosperity and influence.

The coexistence of Muslims, Christians, and Jews in Al-Andalus helped maintain social stability and fostered cultural exchange. Known as *dhimmis*, Christians and Jews retained certain rights under Islamic rule, paying a special tax (*jizya*) in exchange for protection and religious autonomy. While the status of these communities varied over time, periods of relative tolerance allowed for a vibrant interchange of ideas and creativity.

The Islamic Golden Age in Al-Andalus

The Islamic Golden Age in Al-Andalus is remembered as a time of remarkable cultural, scientific, and artistic flourishing. This era positioned the region as one of the most advanced civilisations in medieval Europe. Its achievements were rooted in the Umayyad commitment to intellectual growth, cultural diversity, and architectural innovation.

Scientific and Intellectual Achievements

Translating classical works into Arabic was one of the cornerstones of this period's intellectual achievements. Scholars translated the works of ancient Greek philosophers (e.g., Aristotle and Plato), Roman scientists, and Persian and Indian texts into Arabic. This movement preserved and expanded upon the knowledge of the classical world.

Prominent advances in *science, mathematics, medicine, and astronomy* emerged from Al-Andalus:
- **Astronomy**: Observatories in Al-Andalus contributed to the development of astronomical tables, the refinement of navigational tools such as the astrolabe, and accurate planetary calculations.
- **Medicine**: Figures like Al-Zahrawi (known in the West as Abulcasis) revolutionised surgical practices, contributing foundational texts used in Europe for centuries.
- **Mathematics**: Scholars integrated Indian numerals (precursors to modern Arabic numerals) into mathematical systems, advancing algebra, geometry, and trigonometry.

The *Library of Cordoba*, which housed hundreds of thousands of volumes, became a symbol of intellectual prosperity and attracted scholars from across the Islamic world and beyond.

Cultural and Artistic Flourishing

The art and architecture of Al-Andalus exemplify an unparalleled integration of Roman, Visigothic, and Islamic traditions. Prominent examples include:
- **The Great Mosque of Cordoba**: Renowned for its horseshoe arches, intricate geometric patterns, and expansive prayer hall, it represents a synthesis of artistry and function.
- **The Alhambra in Granada**: This palace complex, built by later Muslim rulers, showcased ornate tilework, calligraphy, and architectural ingenuity.

- **Mudejar Art**: Even after the decline of Muslim rule, Islamic artistic styles influenced Christian architecture in Spain.

Additionally, poetry and music flourished, blending Arabic, Persian, and local styles to create unique Andalusian forms of expression.

Religious and Cultural Coexistence

One of the most notable aspects of the Islamic Golden Age in Al-Andalus was the relative coexistence of cultural and religious groups. Muslims, Christians, and Jews coexisted in what has been dubbed *convivencia*, a period of pluralism where each community contributed to the intellectual and cultural vibrancy of the region. Jewish philosophers like *Maimonides* and Christian scholars benefited from the educational and intellectual environment fostered by Muslim patrons.

This cultural synthesis enriched Al-Andalus, influencing everything from daily life to scholarly pursuits. It also played a crucial role in the dispersion of Islamic knowledge into Christian Europe, especially after the Reconquista began and resources like books and inventions were transferred northward.

Legacy

The legacy of the Umayyad Caliphate and the Islamic Golden Age in Al-Andalus is enduring. The scientific, cultural, and architectural advancements of this period had a profound impact, shaping the Renaissance and the development of Europe as a whole. The works of Andalusian scholars entered Latin Europe through translations, contributing to fields like medicine, astronomy, and philosophy.

Moreover, Al-Andalus serves as a historical illustration of the potential for diverse cultural and intellectual collaboration. The synthesis of traditions and the promotion of learning during this time are remembered as milestones of human achievement.

The relationship between Muslim rulers and Christian kingdoms in medieval Spain was intricate, characterised by both *convivencia* (coexistence) and conflict. Over several centuries, the dynamic evolved through periods of alliance, exchange, and hostility, leaving a profound and lasting impact on the region's history, culture, and identity.

Periods of Coexistence and Cultural Exchange

During the height of Muslim rule in Al-Andalus (711–1031), particularly under the Umayyad Emirate and later the Caliphate of Cordoba (929–1031), there were numerous instances of coexistence with Christian kingdoms. Despite ideological and religious differences, practical concerns often led to collaboration. Treaties and alliances were forged between Muslim rulers and Christian leaders, primarily for mutual benefits such as halting invasions, obtaining military support, or stabilising borders. For instance:

- **Tributary Alliances**: Smaller Christian kingdoms at times paid tribute (*parias*) to powerful Muslim rulers for protection or to avoid conflict. Conversely, Christian rulers occasionally received tributes from weakened Muslim states, exemplifying the fluid power dynamics.

- **Cultural Exchange**: The thriving city of **Cordoba**, under its Muslim rulers, became one of the most advanced cultural and intellectual centres in Europe, attracting scholars from all backgrounds. Christian and Jewish intellectuals collaborated with Muslim scholars to translate texts in cities like **Toledo**, famed for its "translation schools". Ancient Greek, Roman, and Arab knowledge—including philosophy, science, mathematics, and medicine—was preserved and disseminated through these efforts.

- **Multicultural Cities**: Muslim Spain featured cosmopolitan centres where Muslims, Christians, and Jews lived side by side. Although Muslims held political dominance, these cities encouraged the sharing of traditions, language (Arabic), and artistic techniques, fostering advancements in architecture, literature, and more.

Conflict and the Root of the Reconquista

Despite these examples of coexistence, military conflict was a constant undercurrent. The Christian kingdoms of northern Spain—such as Asturias, Leon, Castile, Aragon, and Navarre—viewed the Muslim conquest of the Iberian Peninsula as a temporary occupation and launched efforts to reclaim their territories almost immediately. The **Battle of Covadonga (722)**, where Asturian forces repelled a Muslim army, is often cited as the symbolic beginning of the **Reconquista**.

Several factors drove tensions:

1. **Religious and Political Rivalry**: Muslims and Christians regarded one another as ideological opposites, with religion often used as both a justification for war and a symbol of identity. Political ambitions, however, were equally significant, as both sides sought to expand their lands and influence.

2. **Fragmented Authority**: Following the collapse of the Umayyad Caliphate in 1031, Al-Andalus fractured into a series of smaller, weaker kingdoms (*taifas*), which Christian states sought to exploit. This fragmentation intensified the Reconquista as Christian kingdoms expanded southwards.

3. **Shifting Alliances**: Rivalries within both Muslim and Christian factions often led to alliances that crossed religious lines. For example, Muslim rulers sometimes enlisted Christian forces to fight against rival taifa states, while Christian kings formed pacts with Muslim states to secure advantages over their Christian competitors.

Key Turning Points in Christian Expansion

The Reconquista progressed in waves, defined by major battles and pivotal territorial gains:

1. **The Capture of Toledo (1085)**: Under **Alfonso VI of Castile**, this conquest marked the first significant victory for Christian forces, reclaiming the symbolic heart of Visigothic Spain and further exposing Muslim vulnerabilities.

2. **Battle of Las Navas de Tolosa (1212)**: A decisive coali-

tion of Christian armies defeated the Almohad Caliphate, marking the beginning of the end for Muslim power in Spain. The battle cleared the path for Christian advances into Andalusia.

3. **The Fall of Major Muslim Cities**: By the mid-13th century, key cities, including Cordoba (1236) and Seville (1248), fell to Christian forces, leaving only the Nasrid Kingdom of Granada as a significant Muslim polity by the late 13th century.

The Fall of Granada and the End of the Reconquista

The last chapter of this saga was the **fall of Granada** in 1492, ending over seven centuries of Muslim rule in Iberia. Despite being the last Muslim stronghold, Granada had maintained its independence through diplomacy and tribute. However, the unification of Castile and Aragon under the Catholic Monarchs **Ferdinand II** and **Isabella I** created a formidable Christian alliance determined to complete the Reconquista.

The siege of Granada (1482–1492) saw a mix of negotiated surrender and military conquest. Sultan **Muhammad XII (Boabdil)** surrendered the city under terms that initially guaranteed religious freedom for Muslims. However, these concessions were short-lived, as the Catholic Monarchs soon implemented policies of conversion and expulsion, leading to the eventual persecution of Muslims (and Jews).

Legacy of Coexistence and Conflict

The interplay of coexistence and conflict during this period left an enduring legacy:

- **Cultural Syncretism**: Despite the ultimate triumph of Christian kingdoms, the Islamic influence remains visible in Spain's architecture (e.g., the Alhambra, the Great Mosque of Cordoba), language (many Spanish words are of Arabic origin), and arts.

- **Religious Transformation**: The Reconquista culminated in the eradication of religious diversity, as the Catholic Monarchs sought to establish religious uniformity through the **Spanish Inquisition** and the forced conversion or expulsion of Muslims and Jews.

- **Historical Perspectives**: The period of *convivencia* is debated among scholars. While some celebrate it as an era of tolerance and cultural flowering, others argue that coexistence often occurs within hierarchical structures shaped by political domination.

Ultimately, medieval Spain's history illustrates the complex entanglement of religion, power, and culture, showcasing how cooperation and confrontation can simultaneously shape a society's identity and legacy.

The legacy of Muslim rule in Spain encompasses profound and lasting influences on Spanish culture, architecture, and cuisine, as well as broader European cultural and intellectual development. Muslim rule, particularly during the period of Al-Andalus, left an indelible mark on the Iberian Peninsula, shaping its identity and heritage in ways still evident today.

Architecture

The architectural legacy of Muslim rule is one of the most visible and celebrated aspects. Iconic structures like the **Alhambra palace** in Granada and the **Great Mosque of Cordoba** exemplify the sophisticated artistic, engineering, and aesthetic sensibilities of the Muslim rulers. These masterpieces are characterised by intricate geometric designs, delicate stucco work, arabesque patterns, and serene courtyards with water features, highlighting a deep connection to nature and spirituality (Dodds, 1992).

Muslim rulers introduced elements such as **horseshoe arches**, **muqarnas (stalactite-like features)**, and decorative **zellij tilework**, which later blended into Spanish architecture even after the Reconquista. Many Spanish churches, palaces, and public buildings, such as the mudéjar-style structures, retain clear Islamic influences, symbolising the long-lasting interplay between Muslim and Christian architectural traditions.

Cuisine

Muslim rule transformed Spanish gastronomy by introducing agricultural techniques, crops, and spices that thrive in the Mediterranean climate. The **Moorish influence** brought ingredients like **rice**, **saffron**, **citrus fruits**, **almonds**, **dates**, and spices such as **cumin** and

coriander. These ingredients revolutionised Spanish cuisine, contributing to dishes that are integral to Spain's gastronomic identity today.

An excellent example is **paella**, which incorporates rice and saffron, both introduced during Muslim rule. **Marzipan**, **turrón (nougat)**, and desserts using almonds and honey are also remnants of this culinary heritage. The use of irrigation and farming methods introduced by the Moors further enriched Spain's agricultural output, ensuring lasting gastronomical benefits.

Cultural Exchange and Knowledge

Muslim Spain, particularly during the **Islamic Golden Age**, was a crucible of intellectual and artistic exchange. The inclusive policies of Al-Andalus, which facilitated the coexistence of Muslims, Christians, and Jews, created an environment where knowledge flourished.

Muslim scholars preserved and enhanced the works of classical Greek and Roman thinkers, translating them into Arabic and later facilitating their transmission into European languages. Fields such as **astronomy**, **medicine**, **mathematics**, and **philosophy** thrived under scholars like **Averroes (Ibn Rushd)** and **Maimonides**, who significantly influenced European thought. The system of algebra, advancements in surgical techniques, and studies of the stars in medieval Europe owe much to the knowledge cultivated in Al-Andalus.

Cultural Legacy

The multicultural nature of Al-Andalus gave rise to a distinctive Spanish identity that celebrated diversity despite later attempts to suppress Islamic influence. The combination of Islamic, Christian, and Jewish traditions enriched art, music, and even language. Words of Arabic origin, such as **aceituna (olive)**, **azúcar (sugar)**, and **almohada (pillow)**, remain integral to the Spanish vocabulary.

Significance in European History

The Muslim rule of Spain also acted as a bridge between the Islamic and Christian worlds. The cultural transfer from Al-Andalus to the rest of Europe, particularly through the translation efforts in **Toledo**, played a pivotal role in the **European Renaissance**. This process of knowledge-sharing laid the groundwork for intellectual developments that reshaped Europe.

Conclusion

The legacy of Muslim rule in Spain is a testament to the vibrant cultural, architectural, and intellectual achievements of Al-Andalus. It highlights a period of coexistence and mutual enrichment that reshaped Spain's identity and greatly influenced European history. From the majestic palaces and mosques to the fusion of culinary traditions to the foundational role in European intellectual advancement, the enduring impact of Islamic civilisation illustrates the interconnectedness of global cultures and their contribution to human progress.

Chapter 5

Expansion into Southern France

Impact and Resistance to Islamic Expansion

The Islamic expansion into Southern France elicited immediate and long-term consequences, characterised by dramatic shifts in local governance, trade networks, and cultural exchanges. However, the efforts of the Islamic forces were consistently met with considerable resistance, both from organised regional powers and local populations.

Key cities, such as Narbonne and Carcassonne, fell to Islamic forces during the early phases of their campaigns, becoming administrative and military hubs for further operations (Kennedy, 2007; Harrison, 2007). Narbonne, in particular, became a vital Islamic stronghold in the region of Septimania, serving as a gateway for continued incursions into nearby territories (Tolan, 2013). Despite the initial successes of these strongholds, resistance steadily mounted, fuelled by the disunity and shifting alliances among local powers.

Under Charles Martel's leadership, the Frankish forces played a pivotal role in halting the Islamic advance (Gibb, 1963). Reacting to the incursions into Aquitaine, which brought Islamic forces perilously close to central Francia, Martel mobilised his forces to counter the expanding Caliphate's presence. The culmination of this resistance was the decisive engagement at the Battle of Tours (or Poitiers) in 732 CE, where Martel's forces achieved a significant victory against the Islamic army (Hodgson, 1974). This victory became a turning point, stalling further Islamic advances into the heart of Francia and gradually leading to the Islamic withdrawal from Southern France over the following decades.

Resistance wasn't limited to major battles. Smaller-scale revolts and insurrections frequently destabilised Islamic-occupied territories in the region. Local populations often leveraged the rugged terrain of Southern France, from the foothills of the Pyrenees to the Massif Central, to conduct guerrilla operations and sabotage campaigns against occupying forces (Crone, 2003). Independent leaders and rival factions, such as the rulers of Aquitaine and ambitious Frankish nobility, exploited this unrest to resist Islamic control and reassert regional autonomy (Lapidus, 1988).

Through this resistance, the Islamic grip on Southern France began to weaken. By the mid-8th century, Islamic forces had withdrawn completely, consolidating their control in the Iberian Peninsula instead. However, the presence of Islamic rule in the region, albeit brief, left undeniable effects on local governance, trade, and cultural interaction (Hawting, 2000).

Cultural and Economic Impact of the Islamic Presence

The brief Islamic presence in Southern France sparked significant cultural and economic ripples in the region, some of which persisted even after the withdrawal of Islamic forces. Economically, Islamic control over trade hubs like Narbonne brought closer ties between the Western Mediterranean and the broader Islamic world, facilitating the exchange of goods, ideas, and technologies (Menocal, 2002). Merchant caravans moved between Southern France and Islamic Spain, introducing novel agricultural techniques, architectural styles, and luxury commodities, including textiles, spices, and glassware (Lapidus, 1988).

Architectural influences, though limited in scope due to the short-lived nature of Islamic dominance, included the fortification of strongholds with designs adapted from Islamic Spain (Tolan, 2013). These influences sometimes persisted after recapture by local rulers, blending into the evolving architectural fabric of the region.

Culturally, the interaction between the Islamic occupiers and Christian populations led to a limited but notable exchange of ideas. This period saw the preservation and transmission of classical texts, which had been translated and expanded upon by Islamic scholars. Through sporadic contact facilitated by trade and conflict, fragments of Islamic learning formed part of the intellectual foundations that would later influence the Carolingian Renaissance and broader European thought (Blair, 2000).

However, for local populations, the Islamic incursions were often marked by disruption—social upheaval, displacement, and the destruction caused by military campaigns inevitably left scars on Southern France's political and social fabric (Kennedy, 2007; Harrison, 2007). The return of Frankish control, exemplified by Charles Martel's efforts, signalled a reassertion of local power and Christian dominance, shifting attention away from the brief cultural connection forged with the Islamic world.

Legacy of the Islamic Expansion into Southern France

Although the Islamic presence in Southern France was ultimately short-lived, its legacy lingered in more ways than might initially be expected. The incursions illustrated the extent of the Islamic Caliphate's ambition and capacity, pushing the geographic boundaries of their expansion to unprecedented limits (Hawting, 2000). Moreover, they underscored the critical role of the Frankish Kingdom in shaping the future balance of power in Western Europe.

The victory at the Battle of Tours—and Charles Martel's subsequent status as a defender of Christendom—became a historical touchstone, heralded by medieval chroniclers as a definitive moment of European resistance against Islamic expansion (Ibn Khaldun, 1967). Though later historians have questioned the long-term significance of the battle itself, it remains an enduring symbol of the capacity of European polities to resist external conquest and unite in defence of shared values and interests (Rosenthal, 1975).

Finally, the region's exposure, albeit brief, to the Islamic world, left a latent legacy of cultural exchange, particularly in terms of knowledge transmission and trade ties (Crone, 2003). These early interactions contributed to the longer-term intellectual and economic connections across the Mediterranean, precursors to the more extensive exchanges that would characterise later centuries.

In sum, the Islamic expansion into Southern France, though stymied by resistance and ultimately curtailed, remains a significant episode in the broader narrative of Islamic-European interaction, shaping the geopolitical and cultural dynamics of the medieval period in nuanced and far-reaching ways (Hodgson, 1974).

Key Battles and Siege Strategies

The Battle of Tours, also called the Battle of Poitiers, took place in 732 between Charles Martel, the Frankish leader, and Abdul Rahman Al Ghafiqi, who was the Umayyad Caliphate (Tolan, 2013). It was an important moment for the Islamic conquest of Europe as it dealt a blow to Muslim forces (Kennedy, 2007).

Charles Martel adopted a defensive strategy by positioning his forces on high ground and forming a shield wall to counter the charges of the Muslim cavalry (Blair, 2000). The Frankish infantry stood their ground against the Umayyad assault with spears and swords.

The Muslim cavalry, which had earned fame due to its speed and agility, tried to outflank the Frankish forces, but Charles Martel's disciplined troops did not give way (Gibb, 1963). The Franks also used their superior knowledge of the land to their advantage by utilising narrow valleys and dense forests that restricted the movement of Muslim cavalry.

As the battle continued, Frankish forces gradually improved their position, inflicting heavy casualties on the Umayyad army (Hodgson, 1974). The death of Abdul Rahman Al Ghafiqi further demoralised Muslims, leading to a subsequent withdrawal.

After the win at Tours, Charles Martel continued to pursue the retreating Umayyad forces, making them uncomfortable and preventing them from attacking Frankish territories (Rosenthal, 1975). The Battle of Tours is seen as the point at which the Islamic conquest of Europe was reversed; it halted any further advance by Muslim forces into Western Europe and saved the Christian domains of the Franks and other European kingdoms (Tolan, 2013).

Challenges Faced by Islamic Forces

The Islamic forces' military capacities and strategic choices were tested in various ways as they moved into Southern France (Hawting, 2000). The advancing armies had to deal with difficult terrains and fortified cities (Lapidus, 1988). Local Frankish and Visigothic forces also mounted stiff resistance against the Islamic invaders, who utilised their knowledge of the land and defensive tactics to slow down their progress (Blair, 2000).

The more unfamiliar territory the Islamic forces ventured into, the thinner their supply lines became. This brought about logistical problems and shortages of supplies for them (Rosenthal, 1975). Moreover, soldiers had to endure freezing temperatures and bad weather conditions while still conducting military operations during harsh winters in this area (Gibb, 1963).

Furthermore, the rich cultural and religious diversity of Southern France posed challenges to social integration and governance for the Islamic forces (Hodgson, 1974). For instance, deeply ingrained religious beliefs among the local population differed from those held by their conquerors. This created tensions that needed to be managed carefully through diplomacy (Tolan, 2013).

Additionally, at times, rival factions within these same Islamic forces would cause internal conflicts, leading to power struggles that diverted attention from the main goal of conquests (Crone, 2003). Commanders in the field faced the constant challenge of maintaining cohesion among diverse groups within the army.

The Islamic forces overcame these challenges and established themselves in Southern France through military tactics, diplomacy, and cultural exchanges (Hawting, 2000). The lessons learned from these trials would later have an impact on future campaigns and the long-term effects of Islamic rule in the area.

Diplomatic Relations with Local Powers

In their expansion into Southern France, Islamic forces faced insurmountable challenges; nevertheless, diplomatic relations with local powers played a crucial role in shaping the outcomes of conquest (Tolan, 2013). Complex negotiations, coercion and cultural interaction, characterised the relationships between Islamic commanders and regional leaders (Blair, 2000).

Strategically recognising the need to establish alliances with local powers for successful campaigns, the Islamic forces sent emissaries through diplomatic channels to negotiate with influential figures in Southern France. These talks often involved territorial control issues, trade agreements and mutual defence strategies (Gibb, 1963).

On the other hand, local powers were confronted with the dilemma of either resisting or aligning themselves with the Islamic forces (Crone, 2003). While some leaders saw an opportunity to extend their own influence as a result of the arrival of Islamic armies, others viewed it as a threat to their established authority (Tolan, 2013). This dynamic led to different reactions from various parts of Southern France.

In some instances, diplomatic relations involved giving hostages as a sign of goodwill and commitment to peacekeeping (Kennedy, 2007; Harrison, 2007). The practice helped in building trust between Islamic forces and local powers, thus laying the foundation for future cooperation.

Moreover, further diplomatic connections between the two sides were also made through cultural exchanges in marriage alliances and religious practices (Lapidus, 1988).

In addition, Islamic conquests in Southern France were significantly influenced by diplomatic relations with local powers (Hawting, 2000). The success of the Islamic campaigns in this area depended on their ability to navigate complex political landscapes and forge strategic alliances. Through dialogue and negotiation, the Islamic forces encountered several challenges before they finally settled in Southern France, thereby changing a lot of things about the socio-political landscape of that area.

Administration of Conquered Territories

After the conquest of areas in Southern France, Islamic forces had to administer these territories in a way that would ensure stability and order (Hodgson, 1974). The administration of conquered territories was a strategic affair meant to maintain control while also encouraging cooperation and assimilation.

The conquered territories were governed through a blend of Islamic principles and local customs and traditions (Blair, 2000). Usually, local administrators were appointed to oversee daily activities, whereas Islamic officials managed key administrative functions (Gibb, 1963). This type of dual administration ensured some degree of continuity and familiarity for the locals but, at the same time, loyalty to Islam as rulers.

The management of resources and taxation was central to governing conquered territories. There were attempts made to make tax collection more efficient so that it could be used for military purposes as well as for supporting administrative systems (Lapidus, 1988). Moreover, the imposition of Islamic laws and regulations played a crucial role in controlling socio-economic life among the inhabitants (Harrison, 2007).

Moreover, cultural assimilation was promoted by the Muslim rulers through their policies.

Efforts were made to encourage the adoption of the Arabic language and Islamic customs, albeit alongside the preservation of local languages and traditions (Tolan, 2013). Mosques and educational institutions were established to facilitate the spread of Islamic knowledge and values (Ibn Khaldun, 1967).

All in all, the administration of conquered territories in Southern France struck a fine balance between asserting Islamic authority and accommodating local customs (Hawting, 2000). The governance structures put in place are aimed at promoting stability, fostering cooperation, and ensuring the long-term viability of Islamic rule in the region.

The Islamic conquest of Southern France, although short-lived and geographically limited, had a notable socio-cultural impact on the region that resonates to this day. This period, characterised by cultural exchange, advancements in various disciplines, and the blending of traditions, shaped Southern France's identity in unique ways.

Islamic Socio-Cultural Contributions

1. Art and Architecture

The introduction of Islamic art and architecture left a deep mark on the region. Even though the Umayyad presence in Southern France was not as extensive as in Iberia, elements of Islamic architectural aesthetics—such as geometric patterns, horseshoe arches, and decorative tilework—were carried into local styles, influencing fortifications, religious buildings, and domestic spaces. This stylistic inheritance continued to manifest in Southern Gothic architecture and subtle design elements evident in the region.

2. **Knowledge and Intellectual Exchange**

Southern France benefited from the vast intellectual advancements of the Islamic world, which were transmitted through contact with Muslim-ruled Iberia and the Islamic polities in Provence and Septimania. This period saw the introduction of medical texts, agricultural techniques, and scientific learning—developments that enriched Southern France's intellectual and practical life. Islamic scholars made significant contributions to preserving and expanding classical knowledge, which later influenced the Carolingian Renaissance.

3. **Religious Pluralism**

During the period of Islamic influence, Southern France witnessed an era of relative religious diversity and pluralism. While Christianity was dominant, the presence of Islam introduced a tapestry of beliefs that encouraged cultural exchange between communities. Interactions with Jewish and Muslim intellectuals, particularly through trade and diplomacy, laid a foundation for greater tolerance and mutual respect.

4. **Cuisine and Agriculture**

Islamic agricultural practices introduced transformative techniques and new crops that enhanced local production. Innovations such as advanced irrigation systems, along with the introduction of crops like rice, citrus fruits, and spices, had a lasting effect on Southern French agriculture and cuisine. The culinary landscape absorbed some of these influences, resulting in the unique fusion of Mediterranean and Arabic flavours that can still be appreciated in regional gastronomy.

5. Linguistic Contributions

Arabic, as the language of governance, trade, and science within Islamic polities, left its mark on the local languages of Southern France. Several words of Arabic origin entered Occitan dialects during this era, particularly in domains like trade, architecture, and science. Although often subtle, these linguistic borrowings reflect the depth of contact and exchange during the period.

Enduring Legacy

The legacy of the Islamic period in Southern France endures in several forms:

1. Historical Narrative

The memory of the Islamic presence in the region has continued to influence historical discourse and regional identity in Southern France. Although overshadowed by later periods like the Reconquista and Crusades, this chapter of history highlights a time of productive cultural interactions.

2. Architectural and Artistic Influence

While Islamic architectural monuments in Southern France were largely replaced or repurposed, the influence of Moorish art and Islamic design principles can still be seen in certain features of religious and residential architecture across the region, reflecting a wider Mediterranean and Iberian connection.

3. **Cultural Identity**

The blending of Islamic and local traditions during this period contributed to the development of a culturally rich and diverse identity in Southern France, particularly in regions like Provence and the Languedoc. This fusion has become a part of the region's historical pride and identity.

4. **Intercultural Dialogue**

The Islamic influence, later reinforced by sustained contact with Al-Andalus, has inspired contemporary initiatives aimed at fostering intercultural dialogue. By learning from the region's historical experiences with cultural coexistence and exchange, modern Southern France often seeks to draw lessons for contemporary inclusivity and understanding.

Significance and Reflection

The Islamic presence in Southern France, though brief in comparison to its rule in Iberia, underscores the interconnectedness of medieval Europe with the wider Islamic world. The socio-cultural influences that arose during this period demonstrate how even limited political conquests can leave an enduring mark in art, agriculture, cuisine, and intellectual life. Through these legacies, the Islamic period in Southern France continues to inspire both historical reflection and contemporary engagement with intercultural heritage.

This history ultimately reminds us that cultural fusion—borne from conquest, exchange, or coexistence—has always been a key factor shaping regional and global identities. Southern France stands as a testament to these rich and complex interactions.

Chapter 6

The Byzantine Front: the Balkans and Greece

Introduction to the Byzantine Front

The Byzantine Front was a critical boundary where empires met, and cultures mingled, stretching across Europe, Asia and Africa (Tolan, 2013). The rough terrain of the Balkans and Greece's fertile lands formed a key battleground where the Byzantine Empire defended its eastern border against external threats (Harrison, 2007). This frontier saw military campaigns come and go, and ideas and influences were exchanged between the East and the West. As it became a focus of conflict and interaction, the course of history in this region was determined by the Byzantine Front and left an indelible mark on the territories that it embraced.

Strategic Importance of the Balkans and Greece

Both the advancing Islamic forces and the Byzantine Empire recognised that the Balkans and Greece were strategically important (Lapidus, 1988). Therefore, being at the intersection between Europe and Asia made it act like a link between the Eastern world and the Western. This territory controlled access to crucial trade routes, resources, and communication networks (Tolan, 2013).

The rough terrain of the Balkans made it hard to conquer (Blair, 2000). It had a diverse landscape that included mountains and plains, which provided opportunities for both defensive fortifications and guerrilla warfare tactics (Harrison, 2007). In addition, some key cities such as Thessalonica, Adrianople, and Constantinople were important economic and cultural centres that controlled trade routes that linked Europe with the Middle East (Hodgson, 1974).

Greece was a symbol of prestige and power for any conquering force because of its rich history and cultural heritage (Crone, 2003). The Peloponnese peninsula and the islands of the Aegean Sea were strategically located to provide naval superiority as well as control over maritime trade routes. These territories played a significant role in the defence and prosperity of the Byzantine Empire.

The strategic importance of the Balkans and Greece was not only military or economic but also cultural or religious (Lapidus, 1988). This region was a melting pot of diverse cultures; thus, its conquest meant the spread of new ideas, technologies, customs, etc. Islamic forces who took control over these areas influenced their social fabric, thus paving the way for future interactions between different civilisations (Lapidus 1988).

Early Islamic Invasion of Byzantine Territory

The early Islamic incursions into Byzantine territory marked a significant turning point in the history of the region (Tolan, 2013). The expanding Islamic caliphate began in the 7th century to move towards and take over the Eastern Roman Empire, also known as the Byzantine Empire (Hodgson, 1974). The strategic position of Greece and the Balkans made them primary targets for Muslim conquest.

The conquests usually involved fierce military campaigns and strategic manoeuvres aimed at gaining control over important trade routes and access to valuable resources (Blair, 2000). With its strong fortresses and armies, the Byzantine Empire faced many difficulties from the advancing Muslim forces (Harrison, 2007).

The Islamic incursions into Byzantine territory disrupted existing power dynamics in this area and set up conditions for changing cultural and social environments later on (Tolan, 2013). The clashes between Islamic forces and those of Byzantium shaped the history of the Balkans and Greece, which had lasting consequences on regional development.

These early invasions were the beginning of a number of disputes and power struggles that would shape the relationship between the Islamic world and the Byzantine Empire for many centuries to come (Hodgson, 1974). The conquests and interactions between these two civilisations led to cultural exchanges, economic developments, and religious transformations that influenced the history of this region.

Challenges faced by the Byzantine Empire

The Byzantine Empire had numerous challenges during the initial stages of Islamic incursions into its territory (Harrison, 2007). One such challenge was its vast and decentralised nature, which made it difficult to put up a united front against advancing Islamic forces (Tolan, 2013). Additionally, internal wrangling for power, as well as political instability within Byzantium's leadership, further weakened their capacity to respond effectively to this threat (Crone, 2003).

Moreover, the Byzantine Empire had been in prolonged conflicts with neighbouring powers like the Persians, who had drained their resources and manpower (Hodgson, 1974). This left them open to external invasions and unable to mount any significant resistance against Islamic incursions.

The Byzantine military also faced challenges in adapting to the unconventional warfare tactics employed by the Islamic forces (Lapidus, 1988). The highly mobile and cavalry-based approach of the Islamic armies posed a significant challenge to the traditional Byzantine military strategies, which relied heavily on infantry and fortified positions (Blair, 2000).

The Byzantine Empire also had religious divisions that made it more difficult for them to respond effectively to the Islamic threat (Harrison, 2007). The empire was a mix of different religions. This included conflicts between Orthodox Christians and Monophysites that hindered unity against an external enemy (Tolan, 2013).

In general, these obstacles were major impediments to the effective defence of its territory against early Islamic incursions by the Byzantine Empire and laid the ground for further conflicts in the region (Hodgson, 1974).

Islamic Military Campaigns in the Balkans

The Islamic military campaigns in the Balkans were characterised by strategic manoeuvres, fierce battles and significant territorial gains (Tolan, 2013). Soldiers were well-trained and highly motivated, inspired by their faith and the promise of rewards in the afterlife (Harrison, 2007). The rugged terrain of the

Balkans posed challenges, but these challenges were overcome by adopting tactics used by Islamists (Hodgson, 1974).

Siege warfare was one of the major aspects of Islamic military campaigns (Blair, 2000). The Balkans had well-fortified Byzantine cities and fortresses that were difficult to penetrate, necessitating careful planning and persistence (Tolan, 2013). To weaken city walls for easy entry, Islamic armies used siege engines such as catapults and battering rams (Harrison, 2007).

The other factor that contributed to the success of the Islamic campaigns was their ability to form alliances with local tribes and ethnic groups in the Balkans (Lapidus, 1988). This approach enabled them to obtain help from local people, gather intelligence about enemy movements, and successfully navigate through complex regional dynamics (Crone, 2003). By pooling together local knowledge and resources, the Muslim forces acquired valuable allies as well as information on Byzantine defences.

Moreover, these campaigns demonstrated their commanders' skillfulness and adaptability in a war situation (Tolan, 2013). Through quick, decisive actions, they managed to outmanoeuvre Byzantine forces by exploiting weaknesses in their lines. Feigned retreats, ambushes, and surprise attacks were some of the tactics they employed to disrupt and disorientate the enemy, leading to victories on the battlefield (Harrison, 2007).

The Islamic military campaigns in the Balkans were a clear demonstration of the strategic genius and determination of the Islamic forces. Their ability to overcome obstacles, form partnerships, and outflank Byzantine defences was instrumental in capturing major Byzantine cities in this area (Hodgson 1974).

Conquest of Key Byzantine Cities in the Balkans

The Islamic conquests in the Balkans brought about a significant shift in the power dynamics of the region. Islamic forces targeted key Byzantine cities in the Balkans as a way to establish control over strategic locations (Tolan, 2013). Thessalonica, Adrianople and Dyrrhachium were among these cities that were particularly important due to their economic significance and strategic locations (Harrison, 2007).

Thessalonica, which had thriving trade routes and was strategically located on the Aegean Sea, was taken by Muslim forces after an intense fight (Blair, 2000). The capture of this city opened up access to valuable resources and allowed for further expansion into this area. Adrianople was a major military base for the Byzantines; however, it underwent a long siege before falling to the advancing Muslim army (Hodgson, 1974). Its fall marked a serious blow to Byzantine defences in the Balkans.

Dyrrhachium, a vital port city that connected the Adriatic and Ionian seas, was another target of Islamic conquest (Tolan, 2013). Its capture strengthened Islamic control over sea trade routes and facilitated the movement of troops and supplies in the area. The fall of these major Byzantine cities not only weakened Byzantine authority in the Balkans but also set up Islamic power consolidation in the region.

The overthrow of these significant Byzantine cities within the Balkans reconfigured the political and cultural landscape of this area, thus preparing it for further territorial expansion and influence (Blair, 2000). The strategic importance of these cities played a decisive role in shaping history during the Islamic conquests in the Balkans, as well as highlighting how transformative these military campaigns were in Byzantine society.

Byzantine Society and the Impact of Conquests

The Byzantine society was deeply affected by the conquests of major cities in the Balkans (Harrison, 2007). The fall of these strategic bastions led to significant political, social and cultural changes within the Byzantine Empire. This not only meant territorial losses for the Byzantines but also caused displacement of populations, disruption of trade routes, and economic destabilisation (Hodgson, 1974).

These conquests introduced Islamic governance and administration, thus mixing cultures and traditions (Lapidus, 1988). Muslim rulers implemented new policies and systems that influenced the daily lives of people. By combining existing Byzantine legal practices with Islamic law known as Sharia, a complex legal system emerged which had an effect on social norms and practices (Blair, 2000).

The arrival of Islamic scholars and thinkers also contributed to this intellectual exchange in Byzantium, which led to cultural synthesis (Tolan, 2013). A multicultural environment existed in which various religious groups coexisted side by side with different ethnic groups in conquered territories where traditions mixed with beliefs, resulting in unique societal norms and customs (Harrison, 2007).

The Byzantines also had to reorganise and adapt. This meant that many Byzantine communities were forced to deal with the realities of living under Islamic rule, leading to shifts in power dynamics, economic structures, and social hierarchies (Hodgson, 1974). The integration of Byzantine elites into the ruling administration and military further blurred the lines between conquerors and conquerors, shaping a hybrid society that reflected both Byzantine and Islamic influences (Lapidus, 1988).

Byzantine society demonstrated resilience and resourcefulness during these times of change by adapting to new circumstances while preserving its core identity (Tolan, 2013). The conquests fostered a sense of unity among Byzantine citizens who were determined to fight back against foreign domination (Blair, 2000).

In summary, the Islamic conquests affected different aspects of Byzantine society, thereby creating cultural exchange, social transformation and political realignment, which are complexly interwoven (Harrison, 2007). The legacy of these conquests would leave a lasting imprint on the Byzantine Empire as it moved forward through time (Hodgson, 1974).

Byzantine Resistance and Counterattacks

The Byzantine Empire, in spite of facing a number of challenges from Islamic invasions and conquests in the Balkans and Greece, showed great resilience through their resistance and counterattack strategies (Tolan, 2013). The Byzantine army was famous for its tactical skills and disciplined soldiers who used different tactics to protect their territories as well as recapture lost territories (Harrison, 2007).

One important characteristic of Byzantine resistance was the fortified cities and defensive structures they employed (Blair, 2000). The walls were strong, and they had towers and moats, which made them hard targets for Islamic forces (Hodgson, 1974). Additionally, the Byzantines had skilled archers as well as siege engines that they used to repulse enemy attacks while retaining control over strategic positions (Tolan, 2013).

Apart from being defensive, the Byzantines also launched counterattacks against Islamic advances (Harrison, 2007). Strategic offensives were launched by capable generals leading Byzantine armies so as to retake lost territories or disrupt enemy supply lines (Crone, 2003). These counterattacks often involved a combination of infantrymen on foot or horseback alongside naval forces, which would outmanoeuvre or overpower their adversaries.

Byzantine diplomatic efforts also played a crucial part in resisting Islamic incursions (Lapidus, 1988). Byzantine emperors formed alliances with neighbouring powers like the Bulgarians and Franks to counteract the threat of Islamic forces (Tolan, 2013). These diplomatic moves helped strengthen Byzantium's position and create a united front against the common enemy.

However, despite significant challenges, resistance and counterattack strategies by the Byzantine Empire helped it withstand the pressures of Islamic conquests in the Balkans and Greece (Hodgson, 1974). The Byzantines demonstrated their resilience and determination to protect their civilisation from external threats through military prowess, defensive fortifications, strategic offensives and diplomatic alliances (Blair, 2000).

Greek Culture and Society under Islamic Influence

The culture and society of the region were highly affected by the Islamic conquests in the Balkans and Greece (Tolan, 2013). The interaction between the Greek population and the Islamic conquerors resulted in a significant interchange of ideas, customs, and practices. One of the most notable effects of Islamic rule was new architectural styles and artistic influences (Harrison, 2007). Greek buildings were left with a lasting impression by Islamic architecture, which is characterised by complex geometric patterns and elaborate decorations (Blair, 2000).

Moreover, scholars and philosophers from Islam also brought new knowledge to the area, thus enriching Greek intellectual life (Lapidus, 1988). The Greeks had access to various Islamic texts on subjects such as mathematics, astronomy, medicine and philosophy (Hodgson, 1974). Consequently, this exchange of knowledge led to intellectual growth and innovation within both societies, that is, Islamic and Greek.

The Islamic conquests also affected Greek cuisine (Tolan, 2013). Greek culinary traditions were influenced by Muslims, who introduced new ingredients and cooking techniques, leading to the creation of fusion dishes that combined elements from both cultures (Harrison, 2007). Trade between Islamic and Greek communities also facilitated the exchange of foodstuffs, spices, and culinary practices, thereby enhancing gastronomic diversity in the region.

Moreover, this conquest led to cultural exchanges across religious and ethnic divides (Lapidus, 1988). Marriages between Greeks and Muslims resulted in a mixture of cultural traditions that gave birth to a unique syncretic identity (Hodgson, 1974). This blending of cultures resulted in new forms of art, music, and literature, which reflected the diverse heritage of the area.

In summary, Islamic influence on Greek culture was multifaceted and transformative (Tolan, 2013). It changed many aspects of everyday life, from architecture and cuisine to intellectual pursuits and artistic expression. The Balkans, as well as Greece, still feel the impact of this cultural interaction today, thus emphasising that it is not just about Islam but also about history and culture.

The Lasting Legacy of Islamic Conquests in the Balkans and Greece

The legacy of Islamic conquests in the Balkans and Greece is both intricate and enduring, weaving through the region's history like an intricate tapestry of cultural exchange and transformation (Harrison, 2007). These conquests reshaped the region's political, social, and cultural foundation and left an imprint that subtly permeated its modern-day identity. A rich fusion of knowledge, innovation, and tradition was set into motion, forever altering the trajectory of Greek and Balkan societies (Blair, 2000).

One of the most striking contributions was the melding of ideas and technologies. The Balkans became a crossroads where Islamic and Greek societies shared perspectives, enriching art, science, and architectural practices in tangible and intangible ways. Perhaps the most visible relic of this encounter is Islamic architecture. Functional domes, stately arches, and mesmerising geometric designs punctuated the region's skyline, creating an indelible legacy etched into its structures (Tolan, 2013). Beyond aesthetics, advancements in agriculture reshaped land use, introducing irrigation systems and cultivating novel crops—innovations with lasting economic and societal impacts (Hodgson, 1974).

Language, too, bore the marks of this exchange. Arabic words filtered into Greek, while Greek influence reverberated in Islamic lexicons, creating a linguistic symbiosis that still lingers in subtle echoes (Lapidus, 1988). This convergence wasn't merely linguistic but a symbol of deeper interwoven histories, where identity became layered with shared elements rather than rigid boundaries.

Religion, predictably, stood as a social bedrock profoundly influenced by this contact. Despite persistent tensions, Islamic rule often supported degrees of religious coexistence (Harrison, 2007). The simultaneous existence of mosques and Orthodox churches, though reflective of contrasting beliefs, illustrated a landscape of diversity. This coexistence, while imperfect, fostered an enduring narrative of multi-faith societies—a theme with resonance across historical contexts (Tolan, 2013).

Politically, Islamic governance brought sweeping changes. Administrative systems introduced under Islamic rule introduced centralised governance methods and codified legal frameworks, laying down bureaucratic traditions that influenced regional governance for centuries (Blair, 2000). An emphasis on inclusivity in governance likewise worked to integrate ethnically and religiously diverse populations under shared political structures, fostering cultural pluralism in ways that left echoes in later societal developments (Hodgson, 1974).

In essence, the Islamic conquests were not merely a chapter of domination but a movement of integration, adaptation, and cultural dialogue. This era saw the building of bridges—tangible and symbolic—across cultures, sparking innovation while leaving deeply rooted traditions intact. Its ripple effect continues to resonate in cultural identities, artistic expression, and intellectual pursuits in the Balkans and Greece, shaping the region as a historical mosaic defined by the convergence of the past and present (Lapidus, 1988).

This complex interplay of conflict, collaboration, and transformation reminds us that history rarely walks a straight path. Instead, it meanders and melds, weaving societies together in shared legacies that foster mutual understanding even centuries later.

Chapter 7

The Siege of Constantinople

Background and Context: Setting the Stage for the Siege of Constantinople

For centuries, the city of Constantinople, also known as the "Queen of Cities," was a gem in the Byzantine Empire (Mango, 2005). Its strategic location at the crossroads of Europe and Asia made it a desired prize for conquerors who wished to expand their territories (Hollingsworth, 1991). Byzantine rulers had carefully fortified the city with massive walls and advanced defence systems that had successfully repelled numerous sieges in the past (Brinkworth, 1994).

In the early 15th century, internal conflicts and external threats had weakened the Byzantine Empire significantly from its previous greatness (Macrakis, 2021). Under Sultan Mehmed II's leadership, however, an ambitious Ottoman Empire aimed to take over Constantinople, thus establishing itself as a dominant power within this region (Krämer, 2019). It was about to be a battle between two great enemies.

The gravity of what they were getting into was something that both sides understood as tensions rose and preparations for the siege began. Emperor Constantine XI led his people through fortifying their defences and rallying their troops, while Sultan Mehmed put together a detailed plan on how he would attack. He did this by gathering his forces and using modern siege technology to break down what seemed like unbreakable walls of Constantinople (Gibbons, 1916).

The geopolitical stakes were very high, such that the outcome of the siege would have a lasting impact on the balance of power in the region for decades to come (Lindsay, 2009). The defenders faced overwhelming odds, but their determination to protect their beloved city fuelled their resolve. Meanwhile, a mix of ambition, religious fervour and desire to carve their mark on history drove the Ottomans (Necipoğlu, 2005).

In this context of political intrigue and military manoeuvring, there was all set for an epic clash which would reverberate through the annals of history. The siege of Constantinople was not just a battle for a city but rather a clash of civilisations, a turning point that would redefine Europe and the Middle East map.

Preparations and Strategies: Plans and tactics employed by the attackers

The attack on Constantinople was carefully planned by the assailants, who used both military might and strategic acumen (Babinger, 1992). They understood that the city had strong defences, so they came up with a multifaceted approach that sought to exploit any weaknesses while at the same time maximising their own strengths (Ramsay, 2001). Communication lines were set up to ensure coordination among different units in a clear chain of command, which would help streamline decision-making processes (Shaw, 2007). Intelligence gathering was crucial as it informed them about how the city looked like, its defence systems and where it could be vulnerable (Gaehtgens, 2018).

In terms of tactics, the attackers adopted a flexible approach that allowed for quick adaptation to changing circumstances (Salhi, 2019). They used various siege engines like catapults and trebuchets to break through the walls of the city but also employed sapping techniques, which involved digging tunnels under fortifications in order to bring them down from beneath (Warren, 1995). The defenders of this town were subjected to psychological warfare, such as propaganda and intimidation aimed at instilling fear and confusion among them (Imber, 2014).

In addition, the attackers also implemented a blockade so that Constantinople's supply lines were cut off, and the city was deprived of vital resources, which weakened its resolve (Loukos, 2012). They carried out covert operations like infiltration and sabotage to disrupt the city's defences from within (Turan, 2011). The attackers also used diplomatic moves strategically to gain support from external allies and weaken Constantinople's diplomatic status (Balkan, 2023).

All in all, the preparations and strategies employed by the attackers showed a sophisticated understanding of military tactics and a strategic vision aimed at capturing Constantinople.

The Defensive Measures of Constantinople: The city's defences and how they were utilised during the siege

Constantinople's defensive measures were awe-inspiring. These consisted of massive stone walls that testified to its impregnability; it was fortified with a series of fortifications meant to discourage any potential invader (Mango, 2005). The first line of defence for this ancient metropolis was built in the fifth century AD as part of the Theodosian Walls (Brinkworth, 1994). These walls had double ramparts separated by a moat and were further strengthened with numerous towers and gates (Macrakis, 2021).

Constantinople was also protected by a chain that stretched across the Golden Horn, blocking off the city's harbour from enemy ships, in addition to Theodosian Walls (Livanos, 2017). This chain could be raised or lowered at will and thus provided an extra layer of defence against naval incursions (Sevim, 2012).

The city's defensive strategy also involved a network of underground cisterns that could supply water during a siege (Lotter, 2010). The most famous among these cisterns is the Basilica Cistern, which can hold over 80,000 cubic metres of water and has always been critical for maintaining life in times of crisis within the city (Gaehtgens, 2018).

There were well-trained and well-equipped defenders in Constantinople, including soldiers from various backgrounds and regions. Among the garrison were elite units like the Varangian Guard, known for their fighting skills (Hollingsworth, 1991).

During the siege, the defenders of Constantinople employed a variety of tactics to fend off the attackers. They made strategic use of the city's walls and towers to mount a stubborn defence that resulted in heavy losses for the enemy (Turan, 2011). The defenders also used different types of siege engines and weapons against their enemies' assaults, such as Greek fire, which was an incendiary substance capable of causing great destruction to enemy ships (Necipoğlu, 2005).

On the whole, this showed how Constantinople's defensive measures played a crucial role in repelling the siege and demonstrated its resilience and determination under overwhelming odds.

The Siege Begins: The initial stages of the siege and the first encounters between the two sides.

When Islamic forces approached Constantinople's walls, its defenders were ready with no fear in their hearts (Salhi, 2019). The mighty city had strong fortifications and a good strategic location, making it difficult for besieging forces to overcome them (Mango, 2005). The defenders knew very well that this was an unconquerable bastion of Christian civilisation in the East, and they were ready to fight fiercely in order to protect it (Gibbons, 1916).

The first phase of the siege was characterised by intensive skirmishes and probing attacks aimed at testing the city's fortifications (Krämer, 2019). These initial assaults were repelled with skill and determination by defenders who were led by experienced commanders and boosted by the resolve of the city dwellers themselves (Macrakis, 2021). The advancing forces encountered formidable walls manned by defenders armed with bows, spears, and other weapons (Hollingsworth, 1991).

Nevertheless, they did not lose their spirit as they continued to push forward with the aim of penetrating through the defences of this city in order to win it over (Sevim, 2012). The clash of arms reverberated throughout the land as projectiles rained down upon walls from siege engines, and brave warriors fought fiercely in hand-to-hand combat on both sides (Ramsay, 2001). Each side tried to outdo the other with knowledge of the layout and defensive structures of the city being used to the advantage of those defending it (Imber, 2014).

The siege lasted for weeks, during which time the intensity of the attack increased, with heavy casualties on both sides (Babinger, 1992). The defenders, motivated by their love for their city and religion, stood firm in the face of danger, while the attackers were driven by a desire to conquer and achieve glory (Necipoğlu, 2005).

The first days of the siege demonstrated that both sides were highly skilled and determined. The clash between civilisations and ideologies took place under the walls of this ancient city, thereby initiating a long-lasting conflict that required all participants to be determined and ingenious.

Length and Intensity of the Siege: Examining the duration of the siege and the challenges faced by both the attackers and defenders

The Constantinople siege was a long battle that tested both sides' endurance (Gibbons, 1916). This siege lasted for months, with a non-stop intensity, as two opposing forces fought fiercely to take over this city (Babinger, 1992). The length of this siege alone presented major problems to both parties because their supplies were running low; their morale was fluctuating while their fighters got tired (Salhi, 2019).

The lengthy period it took for the soldiers on both sides affected them mentally and physically. Defenders had to be constantly alert since they were under threat from enemy attacks and bombardments, which meant sleepless nights and constant tension experienced during a siege (Krämer, 2019). On the other hand, attackers had to deal with the logistical difficulties of keeping their forces for long periods in terms of feeding them, clothing them, equipping them, and motivating them while they continued attacking this city (Ramsay, 2001).

As months became weeks, the conflict only grew in intensity, with both sides becoming more desperate to achieve their goals (Turan, 2011). In response to changing tactics from the attackers, defenders had to adapt and strengthen their positions and defences against developing threats (Lindsay, 2009). Meanwhile, the attackers kept coming at them relentlessly until they were pushed to their limits as they sought to break through the city walls and win a victory (Turan, 2011).

The prolonged siege of Constantinople presented challenges that both sides faced, which underscored the harsh realities of medieval warfare. The long-lasting combat took its toll on those involved in it physically and mentally, showing that siege warfare was not an easy thing during medieval times (Necipoğlu, 2005). Despite all these difficulties experienced by everyone involved, the determination and resilience portrayed by both attackers and defenders throughout this protracted siege of Constantinople would be forever remembered in history books about this region.

Key Events and Turning Points: Highlighting significant moments that shaped the outcome of the siege

The key events and turning points during the siege of Constantinople were pivotal in shaping the outcome of this historic confrontation (Hollingsworth, 1991). One such moment occurred when the attackers, led by their skilled military commanders, launched a massive assault on the city's walls, testing the defenders' resolve and fortifications to their limits (Mango, 2005). The defenders, outnumbered but determined, valiantly held their ground and repelled wave after wave of attacks, showcasing their resilience and tactical acumen (Brinkworth, 1994).

As the siege progressed, both sides engaged in fierce skirmishes and strategic manoeuvres, vying for control of critical positions and resources (Lindsay, 2009). The defenders, aided by their knowledge of the city's layout and defensive capabilities, effectively countered the attackers' advances, inflicting heavy casualties and disrupting their siege efforts (Gaehtgens, 2018). Despite facing overwhelming odds, the defenders persevered, thus showing how they remained focused on protecting their city as well as its people (Salhi, 2019).

In the midst of the anarchy and frenzy of the siege, several important events occurred that significantly influenced its course. One such occurrence was when reinforcements arrived for the defenders at a critical moment (Krämer, 2019). This timely intervention provided much-needed support and enabled the defenders to mount a spirited defence against the relentless onslaught of the attackers.

Another crucial turning point was when a bold sortie led by an experienced commander disrupted the attackers' supply lines and caused disorder in their ranks (Necipoğlu, 2005). The besiegers were taken aback by this unexpected action and had to regroup, thus giving time to the defenders to reinforce their defences and consolidate their positions (Turan, 2011).

Ultimately, it was these key events and turning points marked by bravery, strategy, and determination that decided the outcome of Constantinople's siege. The ability of defenders to adjust to changing circumstances, exploit adversaries' weaknesses, and come together in adversity turned out to be crucial in thwarting the invaders' dreams as well as ensuring the survival of the city against all odds.

Siege Weapons and Technology: An exploration of the creative military technology employed during the siege

The siege of Constantinople saw both the attackers and defenders use different types of siege weapons and military technology to try to gain an advantage over each other (Mango, 2005). The trebuchet was one of the most notable siege weapons used by attackers. This was a powerful catapult that could throw large projectiles over long distances (Imber, 2014). Using it, the city's defences were weakened, and its walls suffered significant damage (Lindsay, 2009).

Apart from using siege weapons, the attackers also made use of various technologies in their assault (Salhi, 2019). One such innovation was Greek fire, which is a highly inflammable substance that was often used against enemy ships as well as fortifications (Necipoğlu, 2005). The Greeks are known for their mastery of this weapon; they applied it with devastating impact during the siege, making it difficult for attackers to proceed any further (Turan, 2011).

In terms of defence, Constantinople's defenders used different techniques to strengthen their position. One of the most important developments was the construction of a huge chain barrier across the entrance to the Golden Horn, which prevented enemy ships from entering the city (Livanos, 2017). This defensive measure was vital in stopping enemy naval advances and safeguarding the city against a major vulnerability (Mango, 2005).

The use of siege weapons and military technology greatly influenced how the siege of Constantinople ended. Both sides showed inventiveness and resourcefulness with regard to using new technologies that contributed to making this conflict more complex and challenging.

Human Cost and Consequences: Discussing the impact of the siege on the people of Constantinople and broader implications

The people in Constantinople suffered much as a result of this siege, both physically and emotionally (Gibbons, 1916). The prolonged bombardment by enemy forces led to extensive destruction of homes, buildings, and infrastructure (Mango, 2005). Many civilians were killed or injured during these relentless attacks, leading to great pain and hopelessness among them (Krämer, 2019).

Ramsay (2001) argues that food shortages became a critical issue due to disrupted supply lines and dwindling resources. The scarcity of food and basic necessities resulted in widespread hunger and malnutrition, which worsened the plight of people trapped within the besieged city (Hollingsworth, 1991). Moreover, overcrowding and unsanitary conditions facilitated the rapid spread of diseases, leading to more deaths and suffering for the inhabitants (Necipoğlu, 2005).

The psychological impact of the siege was also profound, as the constant threat of danger and uncertainty took its toll on the mental well-being of those living there (Babinger, 1992). Fear and anxiety gripped the population as they faced relentless attacks by enemy forces with no end in sight (Salhi, 2019).

Furthermore, the consequences of this siege were far-reaching beyond mere suffering by Constantinople residents. The fall of the city had significant implications for the wider region as it marked a turning point in the power balance that shaped centuries to come (Gaehtgens, 2018). The fall of Constantinople to the besieging forces had far-reaching political, cultural, and religious ramifications that reverberated throughout Europe as well as the Islamic world (Krämer, 2019).

The siege had a huge human cost, with many lives lost and communities destroyed. The legacy of the siege of Constantinople is a grim reminder of how war can affect ordinary people and have long-lasting effects on history.

Aftermath and Legacy of the Siege of Constantinople

The fall of Constantinople in 1453 was a seismic event that reshaped the political, cultural, and religious trajectory of the region and reverberated across the globe for centuries. The immediate aftermath marked the obliteration of the Byzantine Empire, which had stood as a bulwark of Eastern Christianity and European civility for over a millennium (Mango, 2005). The Ottoman Empire, under Sultan Mehmed II, emerged as the preeminent power in the Eastern Mediterranean, consolidating its influence and asserting its dominance over Christian Europe and the Islamic world alike (Hollingsworth, 1991). In the vacuum left by the collapse of Byzantine hegemony, the Ottomans transformed Constantinople into their imperial capital, renaming it Istanbul and using it as a cornerstone for their expanding empire.

Religious and Cultural Shifts

The religious complexion of the region was irrevocably transformed by the siege. The capture of Constantinople signalled a definitive point in the gradual Islamisation of previously Christian territories (Necipoğlu, 2005). Hagia Sophia, a symbolic structure of Orthodox Christianity, was repurposed as a mosque, representing both the physical and symbolic transfer of power.

However, the Ottomans also assimilated aspects of Byzantine culture, tradition, and administration, resulting in a syncretic fusion that influenced their governance, art, and architecture (Imber, 2014). This blending produced unique cultural hallmarks that straddled both Islamic and Byzantine legacies, such as the domed Ottoman mosque architecture inspired by Hagia Sophia's grandeur.

Military and Strategic Lessons

On a military level, the siege not only highlighted the effectiveness of superior organisation and strategic innovation but also set a precedent for future campaigns. The use of massive siege cannons, like the one designed by Hungarian engineer Orban, demonstrated a paradigm shift in siege warfare, underlining the indispensability of technology in medieval combat (Gibbons, 1916). The Ottomans internalised and further developed these lessons, using them to devastating effect in subsequent expansions.

European rulers, meanwhile, observed the fall with a mixture of dread and urgency. The collapse of Constantinople was perceived not only as a military defeat for Christian nations but also as a symbolic loss of the gateway between Europe and Asia. It sparked a wave of military and defensive innovation in Europe, with fortifications increasingly designed to withstand the power of gunpowder weaponry (Salhi, 2019).

Economic Ripples

Economically, the fall disrupted the lucrative east-west trade that had flowed through Byzantine-controlled Constantinople. Commerce across the land route to Asia—via the Silk Road—withered under Ottoman control, prompting European kingdoms to intensify efforts to discover alternative sea routes (Babinger, 1992). This economic disruption indirectly catalysed the Age of Exploration, with figures like Christopher Columbus and Vasco da Gama pursuing efforts to bypass Ottoman-controlled trade networks entirely.

Legacy and Historical Turning Point

The siege of Constantinople is frequently heralded as one of the events that marked the transition from the Middle Ages to the early modern period (Lindsay, 2009). It signified the definitive end of the Byzantine Empire and, by extension, the era of the great medieval Christian empires of the East. The Ottoman victory accelerated the waning influence of Eastern Orthodox traditions globally while simultaneously heralding prolonged Ottoman supremacy. This symbolic and temporal milestone underscored the growing tension between Christendom and Islam, which would shape geopolitics for the next several centuries.

Historiographical Debates on the Siege of Constantinople

The Siege of Constantinople has long been a subject of interest for historians, with its enduring significance giving rise to a multitude of historiographical debates. The contentious interpretations of the event stem from its profound religious, cultural, and political implications, as well as the scarcity of unbiased contemporary accounts.

Motivations and Underlying Causes

One of the primary areas of contention concerns the motivations of the Ottomans. Historians like Salhi (2019) suggest that the conquest was driven predominately by Sultan Mehmed II's strategic ambitions to solidify Ottoman territorial supremacy, while others, such as Turan (2011), underscore the religious fervour underpinning Ottoman campaigns. In contrast, further scholarship argues that Mehmed's intent was less about ideological domination and more about securing a geopolitical stronghold that could unify and legitimise Ottoman control in both Europe and Asia.

Military Tactics and Strategic Assessment

A potent theme of the debate revolves around the examination of military tactics. Some scholars paint the Ottomans as innovative pioneers of early modern siege warfare, particularly with their employment of advanced artillery. Others, however, highlight a continuity with Byzantine and earlier Islamic approaches to siege tactics, crediting Mehmed II's adaptive generalship rather than sheer technological supremacy (Krämer, 2019).

There is also discussion regarding the Byzantine defence. Some accounts cast the defenders, under Emperor Constantine XI, as tragically heroic figures crushed by overwhelming odds and global apathy. Others, including Gibbons (1916), focus on internal Byzantine weaknesses, political fragmentation, and an exhausted city-state unable to finance or mount a lasting defence despite its fortified walls.

Religious Dimensions

The siege is often framed within the scope of religious conflict, fuelling debates about the extent to which religion was the driving factor for either side. Orthodox Christian chronicles and Western narratives of the time interpreted the event as a catastrophe for Christendom, painting the Ottomans as relentless agents of Islamic expansionism (Necipoğlu, 2005). On the other hand, some contemporary historians emphasise the pragmatism of Mehmed II's policies post-conquest, including his tolerance of Christian communities within Istanbul, framing the siege as more politically than theologically motivated.

Legacy and Impact

Scholars who assess the siege's legacy sometimes diverge in their interpretation of its wider impact on Europe. For some, such as Lindsay (2009), the fall of Constantinople is the definitive event inaugurating a new order in European geopolitics, functioning as both a cautionary tale and a transformative stimulus for exploration and innovation. Conversely, others argue that the city's decline had been inevitable for centuries, reducing the siege to a final—and predictable—episode in a protracted regional power struggle.

Final Reflections

These historiographical debates underscore the multifaceted significance of the Siege of Constantinople. Whether viewed as a political masterstroke by Sultan Mehmed II, a tragic collapse of Byzantine resilience, or a catalyst for broader changes in warfare, trade, and exploration, its legacy remains a subject of vibrant historical discourse. As historical evidence is reanalysed and reframed, new perspectives continue to deepen our understanding of this pivotal event.

Chapter 8

The Legacy of Islamic Rule in Europe

Introduction to Islamic Rule in Europe

The Islamic conquest of Europe during the medieval period is a significant turning point in the history of the continent. As Muslim armies expanded their territories across the Iberian Peninsula, southern Italy and parts of southeastern Europe, they established Islamic rule in these regions (Holt, 1995). The emergence of Islamic caliphates in European territories brought about a fusion of cultures, ideas and institutions that had a lasting impact on the socio-political landscape of the region (Lindsay, 2009).

The establishment of Islamic rule in Europe was characterised by a complex interplay among military conquests, diplomatic alliances and cultural exchange (Holt, 1995). Muslim rulers implemented administrative systems based on Islamic law, known as Sharia that regulated various aspects of daily life, including governance, property rights and social welfare (Mango, 2005). In addition to new architectural styles such as distinctive horseshoe arches and intricate geometric designs, which continue to define the region's cultural heritage even today (Necipoğlu, 2005), there were also developments in Islamic caliphates within European territories.

Islamic rule in Europe also resulted in religious tolerance and coexistence among different communities. Muslims embraced a multicultural approach to governance, allowing Christians, Jews, and other religious minorities to practice their faiths under certain conditions (Necipoğlu, 2005). This spirit of coexistence promoted peaceful interactions and cultural exchanges that enriched the social fabric of European societies (Gibbons, 1916).

In general, the introduction of Islamic rule in Europe was an epochal period that transformed the political, social and cultural landscape of the continent. The legacy of Islamic caliphates in European territories continues to be felt in the region's architecture, intellectual achievements, and interfaith relations, thereby emphasising the lasting impact of Islamic rule on the evolution of European civilisation.

The establishment of Islamic Caliphates in European Territories

The history of the region shifted significantly with the establishment of Islamic Caliphates in European territories (Holt, 1995). From the early eighth century, Islamic rule expanded into parts of Spain, Portugal, Southern Italy and Mediterranean islands (Gibbons, 1916).

Muslim armies under the Umayyad and Abbasid Caliphate conquered these territories very quickly and established Islamic governance and administration (Mango, 2005). This led to a fusion of cultures as Muslim rulers incorporated local customs and traditions into their rule (Lindsay, 2009).

Islamic Caliphates in Europe were characterised by religious tolerance, which allowed Christians and Jews to practice their faith under specific conditions (Necipoğlu, 2005). This created a diverse and multicultural society where different religious communities coexisted and interacted (Holt, 1995).

The Islamic Caliphates established trade networks that linked Europe to the wider Islamic world, resulting in an increase in goods, ideas and technologies coming from there (Gibbons, 1916). This exchange of goods and knowledge contributed to the development of new industries as well as economic growth in European territories under Islamic rule (Lindsay, 2009).

Moreover, the Caliphates invested in infrastructure projects such as irrigation systems, roads, and architectural wonders, which have had a lasting impact on the urban landscape of these regions (Mango, 2005). Advanced scientific and educational institutions were also set up that attracted scholars and intellectuals from all over the Islamic world (Holt, 1995).

To sum up, the establishment of Islamic caliphates in Europe led to cultural exchange periods, economic growth and religious coexistence. The history and heritage of this region still resonate with the legacies of Islamic rule in Europe.

Economic Impact of Islamic Rule

Europe underwent significant economic changes during its time under Islamic rule through the establishment of different Islamic caliphates. This period was characterised by various principles such as coinage, trade networks and market regulations that shaped Europe's economic landscape based on Islamic economics (Gibbons, 1916). The European-Islamic trade links created by the Islamic caliphates resulted in the exchange of goods, technologies and cultural practices (Lindsay, 2009).

Consequently, many regions prospered under Islam as trade routes boomed and markets flourished (Mango, 2005).

Europe's economy was profoundly affected by the introduction of Islamic banking practices. The financial practices in European territories were influenced by Islamic banking principles that included the prohibition of interest-based transactions and an emphasis on risk-sharing and ethical investment (Holt, 1995). This shift to Islamic banking fostered more equitable and sustainable financial systems, thus contributing to the stability and growth of the economy (Gibbons, 1916).

Moreover, the Islamic caliphates invested in infrastructure projects, including road construction, bridge building and irrigation systems, which facilitated trade as well as economic development (Necipoğlu, 2005). These infrastructure projects not only improved connectivity within European territories but also enhanced productivity and efficiency in various economic sectors (Lindsay, 2009).

Islamic rule in Europe had an economic impact beyond trade and finance into agriculture and industry. In Europe, these techniques led to increased agricultural productivity by revolutionising the agricultural sector with advanced irrigation systems as well as crop rotation methods of Islamic origin (Mango, 2005). Moreover, some of these industries, such as textiles, ceramics and metalworking, made significant contributions towards European manufacturing practices, thereby fostering economic growth while encouraging technological innovation (Holt, 1995).

In general, the economic impact of Islamic rule in Europe was diverse and included trade, finance, infrastructure development, agriculture and industry. The integration of Islamic economic principles and practices into European societies during this time laid the grounds for future economic growth, prosperity and cultural exchange that shaped Europe's development in subsequent centuries.

Social and Cultural Changes Under Islamic Rule

Islamic rule in Europe resulted in significant social and cultural changes that transformed the fabric of society (Holt, 1995). One of the major aspects of this change was the promotion of multiculturalism and religious pluralism. Muslim rulers created an environment where people from different religions and backgrounds could live together peacefully, thus resulting in a rich tapestry of cultures (Necipoğlu, 2005).

Education also prospered under Islam, with institutions such as libraries and centres of learning becoming hubs for innovation and knowledge transfer (Mango, 2005). Scholars from different ethnicities came together to study subjects like philosophy, science, and literature, among others. This exchange had a profound impact on European thought and scholarship (Gibbons, 1916).

The arts also experienced a renaissance during this time, with Islamic patronage leading to the development of architecture, music and visual art (Lindsay, 2009). Islamic rulers constructed grand mosques, palaces and gardens that not only symbolised power but also served as cultural centres. This cultural interaction between Islamic and European societies enriched the artistic environment and influenced architectural styles and artistic techniques (Necipoğlu, 2005).

The social structure further changed with more emphasis on meritocracy and social mobility (Holt, 1995). Education and skills were valued irrespective of one's background, thus creating a more inclusive society where individuals could rise through the ranks based on their abilities.

In general, the social and cultural transformations under Islamic rule in Europe left a lasting impact on the region. It is because of this that Europe still has a dynamic society that is full of diversity, intellectual exchange, artistic innovation, and social mobility.

Influence on Technological Advancements

Islamic rule in Europe led to significant progress in various fields, including technology (Mango, 2005). Among these was the development and spread of new technologies, which had an impact on both Islamic and European societies. One area where Islamic rule played a crucial role in technological advancements was architecture. The introduction of Islamic architecture brought about innovative building techniques such as horseshoe arches, domes, and complex geometric patterns that changed the face of European cities and inspired novel architectural styles (Necipoğlu, 2005).

Additionally, Muslim scholars were instrumental in the field of astronomy, which led to developments in navigation, timekeeping and map-making (Gibbons 1916). The astrolabe, a complex instrument used for measuring the positions of celestial bodies, among other things, was refined and developed further by Muslim astronomers who improved accuracy in celestial observations and helped navigate land and sea routes (Lindsay 2009).

Islamic rule also facilitated the cross-cultural exchange of knowledge and ideas, and technology such as paper making, irrigation systems, and agricultural techniques were transferred from the Islamic world to Europe (Mango 2005). This transfer of information not only increased productivity but also opened up opportunities for more innovations and advancements in different fields (Holt 1995).

In conclusion, Islamic rule had a profound impact on technological development in Europe. By means of idea sharing, architectural innovation, and achievements made within areas like astronomy, this rule has left a lasting imprint on the European technology landscape.

The Effect on Education and Scholarship

Education and scholarship in the region were greatly affected by Islamic rule in Europe (Gibbons, 1916). Madrasas are centres of learning created by Islamic caliphates that became important institutions for knowledge advancement (Mango, 2005). These madrasas were not only religious schools but also places where one could learn various scientific disciplines, mathematics, philosophy and literature (Lindsay, 2009).

Islamic scholars made a significant contribution to education through the preservation and translation of classical Greek texts. Arab scholars translated the works of ancient Greek philosophers, mathematicians and scientists into the Arabic language, which helped preserve this knowledge for a wider audience (Necipoğlu, 2005). This transmission of knowledge had a lasting impact on European scholarship during the Middle Ages and the Renaissance (Gibbons, 1916).

Additionally, there were notable developments in different fields of knowledge by Islamic scholars. In mathematics, for instance, Al-Khwarizmi was among the scholars who made significant contributions to algebra as well as introduced Arabic numerals' use together with the concept of zero that revolutionised mathematics, laying the groundwork for modern maths (Holt, 1995).

Islamic astronomers in the field of astronomy made significant discoveries and advancements in understanding celestial movements and developing accurate calendars. Scholars such as Al-Biruni and Ibn al-Shatir have contributed immensely to the discipline of astronomy, influencing later European astronomers (Lindsay, 2009).

Islamic rule in Europe also encouraged the exchange of knowledge between different cultures and civilisations. In centres of learning, scholars from different backgrounds, including Muslims, Christians and Jews, interacted and collaborated, thereby creating a rich intellectual environment that fostered innovation and progress (Necipoğlu, 2005).

All in all, the influence of Islamic rule on education and scholarship in Europe was far-reaching. The legacy of Islamic learning and scholarship shaped European intellectual development and laid the basis for many scientific as well as cultural accomplishments that followed.

Religious Tolerance and Coexistence

The Islamic rule in Europe brought about a notable atmosphere of religious tolerance and coexistence (Mango, 2005). Unlike the religious conflicts and persecution that often characterised medieval Europe, policies implemented by Islamic rulers promoted harmony among various religious communities (Lindsay, 2009). Christians, Jews, and Muslims lived together in territories under Islamic rule, thus contributing to a rich cultural tapestry (Gibbons, 1916).

Islamic governance fostered religious pluralism that allowed non-Muslim communities to practice their faith without any restriction (Necipoğlu, 2005). Christians and Jews were protected and permitted to maintain their places of worship, like churches and synagogues (Holt, 1995). This policy of accepting religious diversity created a sense of belonging among different faith groups (Mango, 2005).

In addition, the Islamic rulers encouraged interreligious dialogue and cooperation, which resulted in the exchange of ideas between various religions (Lindsay, 2009). Scholars from different backgrounds met in educational institutions such as universities and libraries, where they could discuss issues ranging from philosophy to science and theology (Gibbons, 1916).

This spirit of religious tolerance and coexistence had a lasting impact on European societies (Necipoğlu, 2005). It served as the basis for a more diverse cultural landscape that was inclusive enough to accommodate individuals from different religious backgrounds who could live together harmoniously. The legacy of religious tolerance and coexistence under Islamic rule is a reminder that diverse religious communities can peacefully coexist with one another (Holt, 1995).

Legacy of Architectural and Urban Planning

Urban planning and architectural designs of European cities today are a testament to the legacy of Islamic rule in Europe (Mango, 2005). Islamic rulers brought with them a rich tradition of design and construction that continues to shape the landscape of European cities to this day. The combination of Islamic and European styles resulted in an exceptional architectural and urban aesthetic that portrays a common cultural heritage as well as a history of coexistence (Necipoğlu, 2005).

Islamic architecture is characterised by highly intricate geometric patterns, ornate decorations, and striking domes and minarets. These unique features can be observed in mosques and palaces, among other structures built during the time Islam ruled over Europe (Gibbons, 1916). Some examples include Alhambra in Spain, Hagia Sophia in Istanbul, and the Great Mosque at Córdoba, which are among the many architectural masterpieces that exhibit the beauty and complexity of Islamic design (Lindsay, 2009).

Islamic rule also influenced urban planning, where cities were made for functionality, beauty, and community (Mango, 2005). Streets followed a grid pattern with markets, mosques and public buildings placed in such a way as to create an integrated urban fabric (Necipoğlu, 2005). Urban design incorporated public spaces like gardens, fountains, and courtyards, which provided residents with areas for relaxation and social interaction (Holt, 1995).

The influence of Islamic architectural and urban planning on Europe is not limited to the physical structures themselves. It represents cultural exchange and integration that have enriched European societies and contributed towards a diverse and vibrant urban landscape (Gibbons, 1916). The intermingling of Islamic and European styles has created a visual tapestry that speaks to shared history as well as a legacy of creativity and innovation.

The integration of Islamic and European societies during the period of Islamic rule exemplifies one of history's most dynamic intersections of cultures, characterised by profound mutual influence and transformative exchanges. This cultural blending laid the groundwork for advancements in knowledge, societal structures, and the arts that continue to shape the modern world.

Intellectual Fusion and Knowledge Exchange

The convergence of Islamic and European societies sparked a golden age of intellectual and scholarly activity. Islamic centres of learning, notably in cities such as Cordoba, Toledo, and Palermo, became hubs of intercultural dialogue, where scholars of diverse backgrounds collaborated to preserve and expand the intellectual heritage of antiquity. Through the translation movement, Greek, Roman, and Persian texts—pioneering works in philosophy, medicine, astronomy, and mathematics—were translated into Arabic and then disseminated across Europe. These translated works, along with original contributions by Islamic scholars such as Al-Khwarizmi, Averroes (Ibn Rushd), and Avicenna (Ibn Sina), profoundly influenced European thought. They later provided a foundation for the Renaissance, reshaping Europe's academic trajectory (Holt, 1995; Lindsay, 2009).

The integration was not limited to the transmission of texts; it included methodological advancements. Islamic scholarship introduced rigorous systems of inquiry and mathematical approaches, such as algebra and algorithms, which enhanced European scientific disciplines. These intellectual bridges were not unidirectional but fostered a rich, collaborative exchange that embodied the interconnectedness of these societies.

Artistic and Architectural Synergy

The aesthetic dialogue between Islamic and European societies is most vividly displayed in art and architecture. Islamic architecture—renowned for its intricate geometric patterns, muqarnas (honeycomb vaulting), arabesque detailing, and use of symmetrical spaces—inspired European builders, particularly in cities where the two cultures interacted most closely. Spectacular examples of this cultural synthesis include the Alhambra in Granada, the Giralda Tower in Seville, and the Palatine Chapel in Palermo. These structures seamlessly merge Islamic design principles with local traditions, paving the way for enduring architectural innovations (Necipoğlu, 2005).

Beyond structural achievements, decorative arts such as mosaics, tilework, and calligraphy also found their way into European styles, and elements of Islamic craftsmanship influenced new forms of artistic expression. The appreciation of beauty, paired with functional design, represented a hallmark of the integration of Islamic and European traditions.

Religious Tolerance and Societal Models

In territories under Islamic rule, such as Al-Andalus and Sicily, Islamic rulers implemented systems that allowed for religious coexistence, enabling diverse communities—including Muslim, Christian, and Jewish populations—to live side by side. This coexistence fostered an environment of mutual respect and exchange, giving rise to flourishing multicultural societies where contributions from minority groups were celebrated and utilised to strengthen the collective society (Mango, 2005).

The dhimmi system, which granted religious minorities protected status in exchange for taxes, permitted these groups to maintain their faiths and traditions while enjoying active participation in the economy, governance, and intellectual life. This model of tolerance—while not without its challenges—offered an alternative to the often-intolerant norms of the medieval world, potentially influencing later European ideas of pluralism and societal cooperation.

Enduring Legacy and Memory

The enduring influence of Islamic rule in Europe resonates in diverse facets of modern European culture. Cities such as Granada and Seville retain the architectural fingerprints of Islamic civilisation, while the intellectual contributions of Islamic scholars continue to be foundational in areas like mathematics, astronomy, and medicine. The introduction of crops such as rice, citrus, and almonds, along with technological innovations in irrigation and agriculture, enriches European culinary and agricultural traditions even today (Gibbons, 1916).

The Arabic language has also left an indelible mark on European languages, with countless loanwords—spanning fields as disparate as science (alchemy, zenith, algorithm) and everyday life (coffee, sugar)—serving as subtle reminders of centuries of interconnectedness (Lindsay, 2009).

Historical memory, however, has been layered and complex. While early historical narratives from Europe often cast Islamic rule in adversarial terms, modern scholarship increasingly recognises its nuances, contributions, and the collaborative spirit that defined much of the period. By reframing this history, we gain a fuller picture of how Islamic and European societies coalesced to shape humanity's shared intellectual, cultural, and social legacies.

Conclusion

The integration of Islamic and European societies during Islamic rule in Europe was a multifaceted process that transcended simple conquest or domination. It was a period of exchange, innovation, and collaboration that left a profound mark on European civilisation, shaping its trajectory in ways that are still evident today. From fostering intellectual growth to inspiring artistic endeavours and social systems, the legacy of this integration underscores the power of cultural synthesis in advancing human progress. By acknowledging these connections, we reflect not only on a shared past but also on the enduring potential of cultural dialogue and pluralism.

Chapter 9

Cultural Exchange and Integration

A Tapestry of Civilisations: An Exploration of Cultural Exchange

At the intersection of history and humanity lies an undeniable truth: where civilisations meet, their ideas interweave. The dynamic interaction between European and Islamic societies throughout centuries has left an indelible mark on the development of art, science, literature, and beyond. Unlike a linear transfer of ideas, this exchange was a multifaceted dialogue, one of mutual enrichment and transformation. It is in this interplay that the beauty and complexity of human history unfold – a testament to the shared journey of cultural evolution.

Historical Crossroads and Early Encounters

The seeds of intercultural exchange between Islamic and European societies were planted in the early Middle Ages, a period rife with both uncertainty and opportunity. On one side, the Islamic world flourished as a hub of innovation, trade, and intellectual fervour, while Europe emerged from the shadows of the

Roman Empire's fall, seeking to reconstruct its identity (Holt, 1995).

A prime arena for this interaction was the Iberian Peninsula – a land of merging worlds. Known as *al-Andalus* during its Islamic rule, it became a bridge connecting cultures, with Muslims, Christians, and Jews living in relative coexistence. The city of Cordoba stood as a beacon of this cultural symbiosis. Its opulent libraries, pioneering universities, and awe-inspiring architecture wove together Islamic ingenuity, European tradition, and Jewish scholarship (Mango, 2005).

The Crusades, spanning the 11th to 13th centuries, while violent in nature, paradoxically became a significant channel of exchange. European knights returned from the Middle East with more than war stories; they brought back advancements in medicine, astronomy, and philosophy. Similarly, Islamic societies encountered new agricultural techniques, military strategies, and artistic influences from their European counterparts. These exchanges, albeit born of conflict, planted seeds of intellectual cooperation (Gibbons, 1916).

Trade routes further extended the dialogue between these two great civilisations. From the Silk Road to the bustling Mediterranean ports, goods and knowledge traversed borders. Lavish textiles, exotic spices, and mathematical treatises flowed into Europe, while musical styles, literary traditions, and cartographic methods made their way into Islamic societies. The path of history is rarely devoid of friction, but it's this very friction that sparks the creativity and innovation by which cultures transform and enrich one another.

Islamic Footprints on Europe's Canvas

The Islamic world left indelible imprints on the cultural and intellectual fabric of Europe. As the heart of Islamic civilisation throbbed with scholarly energy, its scholars became custodians of classical knowledge. The ancient wisdom of Aristotle and Plato, long forgotten in parts of Europe, was revived and preserved in Arabic translations. Through cross-cultural collaboration, these texts re-entered Europe, providing the intellectual fuel for the Renaissance and reshaping the trajectory of Western thought (Holt, 1995).

However, Islamic influence was not limited to the realm of ideas; its aesthetic brilliance also captivated Europe. The intricate geometric designs, vibrant mosaics, and meticulously constructed domes of Islamic architecture inspired new artistic styles in the West. Techniques mastered in *al-Andalus*, like the art of tile-making or the pointed arch, would later appear in European masterpieces, subtly reshaping Gothic cathedrals and decorative art. Cultural exchange thrives in adaptation, and nowhere was this clearer than in Europe's embrace of Islamic visual culture (Mango, 2005).

Even the palate of Europe bore traces of Islamic influence. The cuisine was revolutionised as spices such as cinnamon and saffron journeyed across continents. Sugar, coffee, and citrus fruits entered European diets, transforming both everyday meals and culinary traditions. These introductions created not only new flavours but also new customs, such as the coffeehouse culture that would go on to shape European intellectual and social life (Lindsay, 2009).

Beyond physical and material contributions, Islamic culture reframed European social norms. Concepts like chivalry, courtly love, and romantic poetry owe much to Islamic ideals woven with European reinterpretations. The rich layers of influence underscore just how interconnected cultures truly are – neither standing as isolated entities but as vibrant cogs in a shared narrative (Gibbons, 1916).

A Reverse Flow: Europe's Echo in the Islamic World

While Islamic influence on Europe is relatively well-documented, the reverse exchange is less readily acknowledged but equally profound. Through centuries of interaction, European concepts reshaped aspects of Islamic culture. In architecture, Islamic lands adopted and reimagined European structural innovations, incorporating vaulting techniques and spatial designs that enhanced the splendour of their constructions. This infusion of European styles breathed a novel dimension into Islamic architectural expression (Lindsay, 2009).

Similarly, scientific progress in Europe left its mark on Islamic scholarship. Ideas generated during the European Renaissance and subsequent technological advancements intrigued Islamic scientists and engineers, fostering a dynamic environment ripe for collaboration and adaptation (Holt, 1995). The intersections of these influences continued to inspire both regions to push the boundaries of what was possible – an enduring celebration of humanity's creative power.

Artistry in Fusion

Perhaps nowhere was the dialogue between these civilisations more visible than in art. During the Islamic conquests and throughout *al-Andalus*, Islamic and European artistic traditions collided, coalescing into something entirely new. Islamic art, defined by its devotion to intricate detail and abstract geometric themes, borrowed elements from Byzantine and Roman aesthetics. These influences, in turn, diffused back into Europe, enriching Gothic ornamentation and Spanish Christian art forms (Mango, 2005).

Conversely, European crafts were not lost on Islamic artisans. Techniques in sculpture, enamel work, and stained glass made their way into Middle Eastern craftsmanship, offering new pathways for creative exploration. Spanish Islamic architecture, particularly its celebrated use of tile-work and stucco artistry, became a harmonious fusion that balanced the best of both traditions. This cross-pollination transcended aesthetics, fostering a deeper mutual understanding that bridged cultural divides.

Words Without Borders: Literary Exchange

While art shaped walls and canvases, literature shaped thoughts and values. Arabic translators' preservation and adaptation of classical Greek and Roman works were monumental in enabling Europe's intellectual awakening. Works by thinkers like Galen, Ptolemy, and Euclid reached European audiences via Arabic texts, filling the libraries of European scholars eager to rediscover ancient wisdom (Lindsay, 2009).

The exchange went both ways. European poetry, narratives, and philosophies also entered the Islamic world, translated into Arabic, Persian, and Turkish. Islamic scholars didn't merely absorb these works but interpreted them through their own cultural lens, creating hybrid forms unique to the Islamic literary tradition. It was this very performative act of translation that built bridges of understanding across linguistic and ideological divides, expanding each culture's intellectual horizons (Gibbons, 1916).

A Shared Legacy, A Shared Future

History, when viewed through the lens of cultural exchange, reveals itself as a shared canvas – one painted with the strokes of cooperation, competition, and creativity. The cultural symbiosis between Europe and the Islamic world is a reminder of humanity's interconnectedness, where the boundaries between "us" and "them" blur to reveal a richer, more nuanced story. This tale of exchange is not just a relic of the past but a call to action: to embrace diversity, learn from one another, and celebrate the enduring power of human collaboration.

Scientific and Intellectual Exchange

One of the most transformative dimensions of cultural exchange between Islamic and European societies was the proliferation of scientific and intellectual achievements during the medieval period. Islamic scholars, leveraging their unique geographical and cultural position, became the custodians of ancient knowledge while pioneering new advancements across fields such as astronomy, mathematics, medicine, and philosophy (Gibbons, 1916). The translation of Greek, Persian, Indian, and other ancient texts into Arabic laid the groundwork for intellectual assimilation and innovation (Holt, 1995).

Centres of learning like Baghdad, Cordoba, and Toledo thrived as beacons of intellectual activity, where texts written in Greek, Latin, and Syriac were not only preserved but reimagined for a wider audience through Arabic translations (Mango, 2005). This "Translation Movement" knitted together disparate intellectual traditions, forging a bridge between classical antiquity and medieval Europe (Lindsay, 2009). It was not merely an act of preservation—Islamic scholars expanded upon the foundations of ancient knowledge to devise breakthroughs that changed the trajectory of scientific inquiry.

Astronomy epitomised this union of innovation and continuity. Islamic scientists developed advanced observational tools such as astrolabes while refining celestial models and astronomical calculations (Gibbons, 1916). Figures like Al-Biruni and Ibn al-Haytham pushed the boundaries of understanding in optics, geometry, and trigonometry, creating foundational texts that would later inspire the likes of European scientists during the Renaissance (Holt, 1995).

Medicine, too, experienced a profound transformation under Islamic intellectual stewardship. Luminaries like Ibn Sina (Avicenna) and Ibn al-Nafis advanced human understanding of anatomy, physiology, and pharmacology. Avicenna's *Canon of Medicine* arguably became one of the most influential texts in the history of medical education, studied in European universities well into the Renaissance (Mango, 2005). These contributions did not merely impact their owner but also shaped future medical practices and education benchmarks across cultures (Lindsay, 2009).

Philosophical exchanges between Islamic scholars and European thinkers exemplified the synthesis of Greek rationalism with Islamic metaphysics. Scholars such as Avicenna and Averroes bridged theological discourse and rational inquiry, producing systems like Avicennism and Averroism that reverberated through European philosophical development (Holt, 1995). These ideas, often transmitted via Moorish Spain or crusader interactions, laid a foundation for the intellectual revival of Europe during the Middle Ages and the Renaissance (Gibbons, 1916).

Ultimately, the scientific and intellectual exchanges that blossomed during this period created enduring legacies. The collaborative translation, preservation, and innovation of knowledge served as a testament to humanity's shared intellectual heritage, ensuring that Eurasian civilisations were perpetually enriched by their mutual pursuits (Mango, 2005).

Religious Interactions and Syncretism

The Islamic conquests of Europe initiated an era of intricate interplay among religions, resulting in profound moments of coexistence, interaction, and even syncretism. As Islam spread into European territories, it encountered deeply rooted Christian and Jewish faiths, creating complex dialogues that shaped the spiritual and cultural landscapes of these regions (Holt, 1995).

One of the defining features of these interactions was the emergence of syncretic religious practices—an organic blending of Islamic doctrines with local traditions. In certain regions, indigenous customs were woven into the practice of Islam, often reflecting the pluralistic nature of societies under Muslim rule (Lindsay, 2009). For instance, some communities incorporated local deities or rituals into their Islamic faith, resulting in a nuanced and heterogeneous set of religious expressions that celebrated diversity (Mango, 2005).

Islamic governance also fostered moments of interfaith dialogue exemplified in regions like Al-Andalus, where Muslims, Christians, and Jews collaborated intellectually and shared knowledge. Scholarly figures from all backgrounds came together to interpret ancient wisdom, producing an environment that valued mutual enrichment (Gibbons, 1916). This periodic cooperation led to unique philosophical synergies and strengthened mutual respect among faiths (Holt, 1995).

However, interactions between religious groups were not limited to scholarship alone. They also influenced religious thought and practice on a broader scale. Islamic theological arguments, modes of worship, and even architectural styles, such as those seen in mosques and minarets, left enduring imprints on European religious traditions during and after Islamic rule (Lindsay, 2009). Many architectural masterpieces of medieval Europe bear witness to this cross-cultural exchange, melding Islamic motifs with Gothic designs.

The legacy of religious interactions during this period underscores the shared spiritual heritage of Europe and the Islamic world. While tensions and misunderstandings were inevitable, they were frequently offset by cooperative endeavours that generated lasting cultural and theological exchanges. These moments of syncretism and shared understanding ultimately contributed to shaping the contemporary pluralism found within many European societies today (Mango, 2005).

Social Integration and Coexistence

The integration of diverse communities during the period of Islamic influence in Europe fostered an unprecedented degree of social coexistence. With disparate cultural traditions, belief systems, and values intermixed, communities were compelled to adapt and forge bonds of mutual respect and collaboration (Lindsay, 2009).

Trade routes became arteries of cultural and social interconnectedness, enabling the exchange of both goods and ideas (Mango, 2005). Islamic merchants brought exotic spices, textiles, and innovations, while European artisans, scholars, and traders contributed their own goods and customs. This constant flux bred appreciation for diversity, laying the foundation for inclusivity and interconnected societies (Gibbons, 1916).

Despite challenges brought forth by stark cultural differences, efforts toward integration slowly gained momentum as communities learned to overcome misunderstandings. Practical cooperation in areas like commerce, infrastructure, and governance became the cornerstone of coexistence (Holt, 1995). Bonds of friendship and kinship began to emerge, demonstrating how dialogue and collaboration could transcend initial divisions.

Over time, the acceptance of divergent traditions enriched local cultures. Islamic architectural styles were integrated into European cityscapes, cuisines transformed through the melding of culinary traditions, and artistic forms evolved as communities borrowed techniques and themes from one another. This mutual enrichment ultimately celebrated cultural plurality and underscored the strength that diversity brings to societal development (Mango, 2005).

By focusing on shared aspirations, these communities forged lasting legacies of coexistence. Social cohesion improved as diverse groups worked collectively to shape societies rooted in tolerance and mutual respect. These lessons from centuries of social integration continue to resonate today, providing frameworks for navigating challenges in multicultural contexts (Lindsay, 2009).

Conclusion: Long-Term Impacts of Cultural Exchange

The long-term impact of cultural exchange between Islamic and European societies cannot be overstated. These interactions laid the groundwork for mutual enrichment, fostering intellectual, religious, and social synergies that profoundly shaped humanity's trajectory (Mango, 2005).

The blending of customs, traditions, and ideas between these civilisations led to more inclusive societies. Whether through the transmission of scientific knowledge, artistic collaboration, or societal integration, these exchanges created hybrid cultures that celebrated diversity and innovation (Lindsay, 2009). Concepts of tolerance, inclusivity, and intellectual curiosity were embedded into Europe's evolving identity, contributing to the birth of modernity.

Beyond cultural enrichment, tangible advancements in fields like technology, medicine, philosophy, and governance emerged from these interactions. The shared pursuit of knowledge accelerated progress globally, and the cross-cultural appreciation cultivated during this period set a precedent for dialogue between civilisations (Holt, 1995).

In conclusion, the cultural exchange between Islamic and European societies symbolises the enduring potential of intercultural dialogue. By fostering understanding, cooperation, and shared human endeavour, this legacy continues to remind us of the transformative power of collaboration across diversity (Gibbons, 1916). The mosaic of interconnected traditions that emerged from this period exemplifies the strength of unity amidst difference, leaving an indelible mark upon the world.

Chapter 10

Economic Impact and Trade

Economic Interactions

Economic interactions between different regions during the Islamic conquests shaped the trade dynamics of the time. Islamic forces established connections across Europe, North Africa, and the Middle East, allowing goods, ideas, and technologies to move between different lands (Glick, 1999). These economic interactions involved commercial exchanges, cultural exchange, and technological innovation (Sardar, 2014).

These trade routes and networks, which emerged during this period, connected major centres of commerce such as Baghdad, Damascus, Cairo, and Cordoba. They allowed for the exchange of silk, spices, ceramics, and textiles, among other things (Hawting, 2000). These trade routes played a crucial role in linking the regions' economies under Islamic rule and beyond, creating a thriving network of economic activity (M.Factory, 2012).

One of the main features of these economic interactions was the involvement of merchants and traders who journeyed along these trade routes, establishing connections and alliances with their counterparts in far-off lands (Abun-Nasr, 2011). These merchants not only facilitated the exchange of goods but also acted as cultural emissaries, imparting knowledge and ideas that contributed to that period's intellectual and artistic efflorescence (Griffiths, 2021).

Economic interactions during the Islamic conquests resulted in the development of sophisticated currency and banking systems. These systems made it possible for trade and finance to be carried out smoothly across different regions (Khan, 2014). Moreover, marketplaces were established in cities along trading routes, and trade fairs were held there. Consequently, goods could be exchanged easily, creating vibrant economies that attracted merchants from all over the world (Cohen, 1994).

In general terms, economic interactions during the Islamic conquests played a significant role in enhancing economic prosperity, cultural exchange and technological progress within Islamic territories (Lewis, 1993). These interactions laid a foundation for today's interconnected globe, where international trade continues to transcend borders, thereby bringing people together into one global marketplace (Lindsay, 2008).

Trade Routes and Networks

The Islamic conquests in Europe led to the creation of trade routes and networks that played a major role in shaping economic interactions between regions (Burns, 2009). These networks facilitated the exchange of goods, ideas, and cultures, creating a vibrant economic landscape that spurred growth and prosperity (Cerulli, 2011).

The Silk Road was one of the most important trade routes connecting the Mediterranean region with the Far East (Wang, 1997). This route allowed for luxury goods like silk, spices, and precious metals to be traded, enriching merchants and traders along its path (Hansen, 2012). The Mediterranean Sea also had maritime routes that played a vital role in facilitating trade between Europe, Asia, and Africa (Philipp, 2011).

These commercial networks spanned vast distances due to the development of these trade routes (Wilkinson, 2018). Merchants formed partnerships and alliances, creating a web of connections that allowed for the efficient exchange of goods and services (Courcy, 2019). Not only did these networks facilitate trade, but they also promoted cultural exchange and communication among civilisations (Gerlach, 2015).

This led to cities on the trade routes becoming more important as centres of commerce.

Trading hubs such as Constantinople, Cordoba and Venice became busy cities where goods from far regions were bought, sold and exchanged (Baker, 2004). The growth of these cities was fuelled by the flow of wealth from trade, leading to the establishment of sophisticated markets, bazaars and trading posts (Hodgson, 1974).

Moreover, advances in transport and communication also contributed to the success of trade routes and networks during the Islamic conquests (Khan, 2014). Caravans, ships and camels were used to transport goods over long distances. Furthermore, secure transactions and trade agreements were facilitated by the development of banking systems as well as commercial laws (El-Tobgui, 2016).

In conclusion, the establishment of trade routes and networks during the Islamic conquests in Europe transformed the economic landscape of this region (Devine, 2010). These networks led to the exchange of goods and ideas that fostered cultural exchange, thereby contributing to growth and prosperity across European societies and beyond (Elias, 2001).

The Mediterranean Trade's Significance

The Mediterranean region has, for a long time, been the mainstay of trade and commercial activities, bringing together different cultures and enabling the exchange of commodities, information, and technologies (Pomeranz, 2000). The Mediterranean Sea was an active route for merchants from civilisations such as Greece, Romans, and Phoenicians because it is located between two continents (Abu-Lughod, 1989).

Furthermore, the importance of Mediterranean trade was magnified during the period of Islamic conquests in Europe (Meyer, 2006). Muslim traders recognised that numerous economic opportunities within this area could be tapped into through existing commercial networks (Dodge, 2007). This created new avenues for commerce and cultural interactions, leading to economic growth across the Mediterranean basin (Gohar, 2013).

The movement of goods between East and West increased significantly as Islamic powers took control over major ports and trade routes (Harrison, 2014). European markets received luxury items like silk, spices, ceramics, and textiles, among others, which improved their economies, thus enhancing the lives of many people (Davis, 2001). The introduction of new products and inventions led to the development of vibrant marketplaces and trading centres, thereby stimulating business activities in this area (Khalidi, 1998).

Furthermore, the Islamic conquests encouraged entrepreneurship and business among traders, who facilitated trade across the Mediterranean (Naff, 1985). They formed networks of exchange that stretched from the coasts of North Africa to the harbours of Italy and Spain, creating a complex system of economic interdependence that was advantageous to all parties involved (Gill, 2012).

In general, it is important to emphasise the significance of Mediterranean trade during the period of Islamic conquests (Michael, 2009). It acted as a stimulus for economic growth, cultural diffusion and technological progress, which laid a foundation for future flourishing commercial networks that would shape Europe's and the Islamic world's destiny (Harrison, 2014).

Commerce in the wake of Islamic Conquests

According to Glick (1999), commerce was significantly impacted by the Islamic conquests in all the regions they conquered. The Islamic forces took control of important trading hubs and established new economic networks through territorial expansion into key trade routes and strategic locations (Yıldız, 2020). This resulted in changes in the movement of goods and resources as well as influencing economic practices and policies (Rosenthal, 1992).

The Islamic conquests enhanced trade and cultural exchange between different regions, thereby connecting previously isolated markets, which facilitated commodity exchange, idea sharing and technology transfer (Gordon, 2001). Particularly under Islamic rule, Mediterranean trade thrived with goods moving between Europe, Africa, Asia and the Islamic world (Pomeranz, 2000).

One of the most significant economic impacts of Islam's conquests was the establishment of stable and secure trade routes (Khan, 2014). The building of roads, bridges and caravanserais by Muslim rulers facilitated the movement of goods while providing security for merchants who travelled over long distances (Jaboori, 2015). This infrastructure supported growth in long-distance trade and contributed to prosperity among cities along these paths (Lehmann, 2006).

Additionally, the Islamic conquests introduced new economic practices and technologies that impacted commercial activities in the conquered areas (Baker, 2004). The Islamic traders brought advanced accounting systems, banking services, and credit facilities, which changed how transactions were done and thus promoted trade (El-Fadl, 1998). For instance, paper money simplified trade and enabled traders to engage in business more efficiently (Glick, 1999).

The influence of Islamic conquests on commerce was diverse and extensive (Naff, 1985). By gaining control over key trading routes, encouraging economic interactions between different regions and innovating trading techniques, the Islamic conquests had a great impact on the economic structure of their conquered lands (Sardar, 2014).

Cities as Trade Centres

Cities were very important as trade centres during the Islamic conquests in Europe (Fowler, 2001). Cities became vibrant economic hubs that connected various regions and facilitated the exchange of goods and ideas with the spread of Islam (Cohen, 1994). These urban centres acted as commercial focal points, attracting a variety of merchants from different backgrounds and thus creating a lively marketplace (Griffiths, 2021).

The cities' strategic location on trade routes helped to promote the flow of goods and services, leading to economic growth and cultural exchange (El-Tobgui, 2016). The city dwellers were involved in different sectors, including handicrafts or even farming, which contributed to the wealth and prosperity of these urban centres (Hodgson, 1974). In bustling streets, markets flourished, with products from far away being sold alongside those from close by (Devine, 2010).

As trade networks expanded, cities became cosmopolitan melting pots where various cultures met and mixed (Sardar, 2014). The diversity of urban populations resulted in a rich tapestry of traditions and practices that influenced the development of trade and commerce (Harrison, 2014). In these cities, merchants from far-off lands found an inviting atmosphere in which they could conduct business and establish contacts with local traders (Cohen, 1994).

The existence of markets in towns acted as important economic engines propelling the exchange of goods and services between sellers and buyers (Gill, 2012). These bustling centres of trade were more than just places for purchasing or vending commodities; they also served as social arenas where people congregated to interact, bargain or engage in business activities (Lehmnn, 2006). The dynamism displayed by city markets was indicative of the nature of trade during this period (Cohen, 1994).

The economic landscape of the Islamic conquests in Europe was shaped by cities as centres of trade (Philipp, 2011). Urban environments provided the necessary infrastructure and resources that promoted commercial activities, thus enabling the movement of goods and economic development (Fowler, 2001). Cities played a significant role in integrating diverse societies and developing a dynamic economy through commerce and cultural exchange (Griffiths, 2021).

Merchants and Marketplaces

Medieval European marketplaces were made vibrant by merchants (Khan, 2014). These enterprising people facilitated the exchange of goods and services across the continent through intricate networks of trade routes connecting cities as well as regions (Gohar, 2013).

Merchants used knowledge about local markets, quality products, and current trading trends to shape their era's economic landscape (Rosenthal, 1992). They acted as intermediaries between producers and consumers, negotiating prices, arranging contracts and facilitating transactions that kept commerce flowing smoothly (El-Fadl, 1998).

These marketplaces were diverse, with vendors from different cultural and racial backgrounds (Meyer, 2006). They brought not only goods but also thoughts, discoveries and practices from faraway lands, which made European society richer (Lindsay, 2008).

Merchants were clever business people who knew how to navigate the difficulties of trade, such as changing prices, fluctuating demand and political instability (Glick, 1999). How successful they were depended on their ability to create and maintain relationships with other merchants, suppliers and customers that promoted trustworthiness in trading (Davis, 2001).

In these vibrant marketplaces, the sellers displayed their merchandise at bustling squares and stalls where one could find both exotic and ordinary items, luxurious or basic products (Harrison, 2014). These hubs of commerce attracted many customers who wanted to buy the latest products from nearby or distant places, thus fueling a culture of consumption and exchange that stimulated economic growth and prosperity (Khalidi, 1998).

The medieval merchants and their markets have left a lasting impact, which has shaped the global economy as we know it today (Meyer, 2006). This is because they had an entrepreneurial spirit that was full of innovation and adaptability, which shows that trade and commerce are still powerful forces in shaping our world (Philipp, 2011).

Agricultural and Industrial Production

Islamic rule in Europe brought about significant advancements in agricultural and industrial production (Sardar, 2014). The introduction of new crops, irrigation techniques, and farming revolutionised the region's agricultural landscape (Griffiths, 2021). Islamic rulers implemented innovative practices that improved yields and overall productivity, leading to economic growth and prosperity in the conquered territories (Khan, 2014).

One of the key contributions of Islamic rule was the introduction of new crops such as citrus fruits, rice, and cotton that flourished under Mediterranean climatic conditions (Abun-Nasr, 2011). These crops not only diversified agricultural production but also boosted trade and commerce since surplus produce could be exported to other regions (Cohen, 1994). Moreover, sophisticated irrigation technologies like qanats and water wheels were introduced to maximise scarce water resources for increased crop yields (El-Fadl, 1998).

Concerning industrial production, Islamic rule facilitated the evolution of new technologies and craftsmanship (Yıldız, 2020). In cities such as Cordoba, Toledo and Palermo, artisans and craftsmen excelled in many industries, including textiles, leatherwork, ceramics and metalwork (Naff, 1985). These industries were supported by Islamic rulers through workshops, guilds and markets that created a vibrant economy based on skilled craftsmanship (Lehmnn, 2006).

Moreover, the knowledge exchange between Christian and Islamic communities resulted in cross-cultural innovations and advancements in industrial production (Dodge, 2007). Muslim artists brought their expertise in intricate design patterns, geometric motifs and architectural techniques that influenced the artistic styles of this area (Meyer, 2006). This cultural exchange produced a rich tapestry of artistic expression, which still shapes European societies today (Pomeranz, 2000).

On the whole, agricultural and industrial production under Islamic rule in Europe laid the foundation for economic prosperity and cultural development in this region (Griffiths, 2021). The combination of Islamic and local traditions created a dynamic environment that encouraged innovation and trade growth, thus leaving an indelible mark on European societies to date.

Currency And Banking Systems

In Europe, the currency and banking systems were instrumental in enhancing economic activities and promoting trade across the regions affected by the Islamic conquests (Baker, 2004). The expansion of Islamic rule led to the emergence of new currencies as well as banking practices that influenced the economic landscape and contributed to a more integrated financial system (Glick, 1999).

The Islamic gold dinar and silver dirham were introduced as standard currencies for trade and commerce in one important development (Harrison, 2014). These coins circulated widely, hence providing an acceptable medium of exchange which promoted stability in business transactions (El-Fadl, 199standardisationdisation of currency facilitated cross-border trade and enhanced economic interactions between regions under Islamic rule (Khan, 2014).

A standardised currency, the Islamic banking system also played a key role in supporting economic activities (Davis, 2001). The principles governing Islamic banking based on Sharia law prohibited riba or interest charges while encouraging risk-sharing and ethical investments (Naff, 1985). It was this system that promoted a fairer financial environment where confidence existed among traders and merchants.

Hence, Islamic banking practices, such as Hawala, a system of transferring funds without the physical movement of money, facilitated international trade and financial transactions (Glick, 1999). This informal banking system was crucial in enhancing economic activities and ensuring capital flows across regions (Sardar, 2014).

Moreover, different economic policies and regulations were implemented by Islamic leaders to control the financial system (Meyer, 2006). Currency circulation monitoring was put in place, as well as counterfeit prevention measures, with fair trade promotion being another regulation (Burns, 2009). Through these regulations, the Islamic authorities aimed to create a conducive environment for economic growth and prosperity (Cohen, 1994).

Overall, the currency and banking systems of the Islamic world played a crucial role in shaping the economic landscape of the regions affected by the Islamic conquests (Philipp, 2011). These systems not only facilitated trade and commerce but also promoted financial stability, fostering economic growth and prosperity across the newly conquered territories (Pomeranz, 2000).

Economic Policies and Regulations

The economic policies and regulations introduced during the Islamic conquests in Europe significantly influenced the development of trade, commerce, and resource management throughout the region. These policies were carefully designed to create efficient economic systems, promote equitable wealth distribution, and foster regional prosperity (Cohen, 1994). A hallmark of Islamic governance during this period was its pragmatic approach to integrating local economies into a broader network of exchange while maintaining stability and trust across diverse communities (Griffiths, 2021).

One fundamental aspect of these economic policies was the regulation of trade and commerce. Islamic rulers enacted detailed laws aimed at protecting traders, ensuring fair practices, and maintaining the quality of goods and services (El-Fadl, 19standardisingardising trade practices and enforcing transparency in transactions, they sought to eliminate fraud and enhance trust in local and international markets (Khan, 2014). These measures encouraged long-distance trade, especially across critical routes such as the Mediterranean and trans-Saharan networks, leading to the creation of thriving commercial hubs in cities such as Córdoba and Toledo (Glick, 1999).

Equally significant were the tax systems implemented by Islamic authorities, which were both systematic and adaptable (Meyer, 2006). Two primary categories of taxation, the *jizya* (levied on non-Muslims) and *zakat* (an alms tax for Muslims), not only generated revenue for public expenditures but also reflected a carefully balanced fiscal policy rooted in Islamic principles (Naff, 1985). Agricultural lands were taxed according to their productivity, fostering better land management practices (Yıldız, 2020). The revenues thus collected funded investments in public works such as roads, irrigation systems, and education while maintaining a steady flow of income for administrative purposes.

Monetary policy was another critical innovation under Islamic governance, contributing to the establishment of robust financial systems. Islam standardised currency by introducing coins that promoted trade consistency across their domains (Devine, 2010). The regulation of precious metals and exchange rates facilitated trustworthy and efficient transactions, while early forms of credit and financial tools, including letters of credit (*sakk*), laid the groundwork for modern banking systems (Courcy, 2019). These innovations in monetary management helped create dynamic economies where merchants, artisans, and local farmers could participate more actively in regional and international trade.

Additionally, Islam emphasised agricultural development as the backbone of economic prosperity. Through investments in advanced irrigation techniques, crop diversification, and land use assessments, they enhanced productivity and mitigate risks posed by environmental challenges (Gohar, 2013). These agricultural policies ensured food security and surplus trade, reinforcing the stability of the economy (Philipp, 2011).

In sum, the Islamic conquests brought a sophisticated, multilayered approach to economic regulations that intertwined governance, commerce, and resource management. By focusing on fairness, innovation, and inclusivity, these policies not only bolstered the economy during their rule but also left enduring legacies for future generations (Baker, 2004).

Conclusion: Assessing the Long-Term Economic Effects

The long-term economic impact of the Islamic conquests in Europe has been profound. The economic framework introduced under Islamic governance significantly shaped Europe's commercial and agricultural landscapes and contributed to broader socio-economic transformations (Meyer, 2006). By fostering interconnected trade networks, advancing agricultural practices, and instituting fair systems of taxation and resource allocation, the Islamic rulers set critical precedents that directly influenced Europe's economic structures.

One of the lasting contributions was the integration of Europe into a diverse and expansive trade network stretching across North Africa, the Middle East, and Asia (Glick, 1999).

This integration expanded the exchange of goods, technologies, and ideas, setting the stage for Europe's later economic resurgence during the High Middle Ages and beyond (Rosenthal, 1992). It also established long-term commercial hubs in regions under Islamic influence, which became focal points for international trade.

Innovations in agriculture, such as advanced irrigation techniques and the introduction of new crops (including citrus fruits, sugarcane, and cotton), transformed European agricultural capacities (Gohar, 2013). These practices not only increased yields but also diversified economies, reducing dependency on singular industries or unreliable farming methods (Davis, 2001). The resulting agricultural prosperity played a vital role in facilitating Europe's sustained population urbanisation in subsequent centuries.

Furthermore, the Islamic emphasis on standardisation and financial tools, such as credit systems, introduced a framework for modern banking that supported economic stability and encouraged entrepreneurship (Griffiths, 2021). The trust-based systems of trade and investment that developed under Islamic administrations influenced emerging European practices in commerce and finance, particularly during the Renaissance (Sardar, 2014).

Lastly, the Islamic rulers' judicious balance between state regulation and market freedom reshaped economic governance. By crafting policies that curbed monopolies and enforced trade-harmonised taxation structures, they demonstrated how regulatory frameworks could sustain economic growth without stifling innovation (El-Fadl, 1998). This legacy left a significant blueprint for later European states in the realm of economic management.

In conclusion, the economic policies and regulations implemented during the Islamic conquests stabilised and enhanced the prosperity of regions under their rule but also laid the groundwork for Europe's eventual economic transformation in the centuries to come. By weaving together trade, agriculture, taxation, and monetary regulation, these strategies helped build a vibrant and interconnected economic system whose ripple effects continue to influence economic thought and practice today (Elias, 2001).

Chapter 11

Religious Shifts and Interactions

Religious dynamics in medieval Europe were a complex and multifaceted social phenomenon. During this period, the continent was characterised by the diffusion and interaction of various spiritual traditions, with Islam and Christianity being the most prominent (Smith, 2011). These two religions, along with Judaism, constituted the central religious landscape of that time, influencing the beliefs, practices, and identities of European people (MacCulloch, 2011).

The spread of Islam and Christianity in Europe was a significant part of the religious dynamics of the medieval period. Christianity, established in Europe since the Roman Empire, continued to expand and evolve during this time (Armstrong, 2006). The conversion of European kingdoms to Christianity, the establishment of monastic communities, and the Church's influence shaped the religious landscape across the continent (Horsley, 2012).

On the other hand, Islam's spread into Europe brought about another religion that challenged Christian dominance.

Muslims were introduced to Europe by the Islamic conquest of the Iberian Peninsula, Sicily, and parts of Southern Italy.

Consequently, both Muslim and Christian societies coexisted (Meyer, 2006). This resulted in cultural exchange between them, intellectual dialogue, and sometimes conflict (Glick, 1999).

The religious dynamics of medieval Europe did not only revolve around Islam and Christianity. Jewish communities also played a significant role in the religious landscape, which experienced periods of integration as well as persecution (Baker, 2004). The society, culture, and politics of the time were shaped by the various interactions among Muslims, Christians, and Jews, leading to diversity in religion (Horsley, 2012).

In general, the religious dynamics of medieval Europe involved multiple religions that interacted with one another through competition or coexistence. This complex and ever-changing landscape gave rise to European identities and beliefs that have influenced its history to this day (MacCulloch, 2011).

Spread of Islam and Christianity in Europe

The spread of Islam in Europe was a complex process that unfolded over centuries, shaped by political, social, and cultural factors (Meyer, 2006). The Islamic conquests of the early medieval period played a significant role in introducing Islam to the continent. These conquests brought new rulers and societies that practised Islam, leading to the establishment of Islamic states in regions such as Spain, Sicily, and parts of Southern Italy (Glick, 1999).

Contrary to this religion's arrival in Europe, Christianity had been dominant for many years. Missionary activities were among the forces behind Christian expansion. The conversion of rulers and elites and the establishment of monasteries and churches were other factors that contributed to the spread of Christianity (Armstrong, 2006). In this regard, when the Roman Empire converted to Christianity during the fourth century, it marked a turning point for its further expansion on European soil (Horsley, 2012).

Smith (2011) notes that interactions between Muslims and Christians in Europe during the medieval period were characterised by both conflict and cooperation. For instance, Islamic rule in Spain led to a lively cultural exchange among Muslims, Christians, and Jews, who made significant strides in art, architecture, science, and philosophy (Meyer, 2006). In Sicily, under Norman rule, Christian, Muslim, and Jewish communities lived together, influencing each other's cultural and intellectual traditions (Elias, 2001).

The spread of Islam and Christianity across Europe had far-reaching consequences for the religious landscape of the continent. This resulted in a pluralistic society with different religious practices and beliefs (MacCulloch, 2011). The interactions between Muslims, Christians, and Jews formed a complex tapestry of cultural expression and intellectual exchange that shaped European civilisation's development even today (Horsley, 2012).

Interactions between Muslims, Christians, and Jews

During the medieval period in Europe, interactions between Muslims, Christians, and Jews were complex and multifaceted (Armstrong, 2006). These three religious communities coexisted in various regions, leading to a rich tapestry of cultural exchange and intellectual dialogue (Baker, 2004). While there were instances of conflict and tension, there were also periods of cooperation and mutual influence (Meyer, 2006). This chapter explores the dynamics of interaction between Muslims, Christians, and Jews, highlighting the diversity and complexity of religious relationships during this period.

Muslims lived together with Christians as well as Jews in many parts of Europe during medieval times, thus allowing them to come into contact with each other, thereby promoting cultural exchange (Elias 2001). In addition, they could interact through trade routes, academic institutions, and urban centres, which acted as points where different religions met for discussions (Smith 2011). Such interactions often resulted in exposure to new ideas or practices that led to syncretism among religions across cultures (MacCulloch 2011).

One area that was central to the relationships among Muslims, Christians, and Jews was their sharing of religious ideas and philosophical thoughts (Baker 2004). Scholars from all three communities engaged in intellectual debates and discussions drawing on ancient Greek, Roman, and Persian thinkers' works (Glick 1999). Muslim scholars translated Greek texts into Arabic, preserving this knowledge for Europe.

This led to the spread of Islamic knowledge in Europe through Christian and Jewish scholars who also translated Arabic texts into Latin (Meyer, 2006).

Smith (2011) also observed interfaith dialogue and cooperation in art, architecture, and music. Muslims, Christians and Jews shared artistic techniques with each other, leading to the development of a rich visual culture that blended different traditions together (Elias, 2001). Architectural styles from the Islamic world influenced Christian and Jewish building practices, resulting in syncretic religious spaces that reflected a common cultural heritage (Baker, 2004).

However, despite such interactions, there were periods of tension and conflict among Muslims, Christians, and Jews (Armstrong, 2006). Religious differences, as well as political rivalries, often resulted in violence or persecution whereby, at various times, each community was discriminated against or persecuted (MacCulloch, 2011). The reconquest of Spain by Christians from

Muslims, the crusades by Christians against Muslims, and the Spanish Inquisition are some instances where interreligious relations during medieval Europe were characterised by turbulence (Elias, 2001).

The relationships between Muslims, Christians and Jews in medieval Europe were complex mixtures of cooperation alongside conflicts.

The chapter underlines the different types of relationships that existed between these religious communities, emphasising the significance of appreciating the subtleties that characterised religious contacts in shaping medieval Europe's cultural outlook (Glick 1999).

Religious Tolerance and Intolerance

The medieval era in Europe was characterised by a complex interplay of religious tolerance and intolerance among Muslims, Christians, and Jews (MacCulloch, 2011). There were instances of mutual respect and peaceful coexistence, as well as instances of friction and conflict based on religious differences (Armstrong, 2006). The concept of religious tolerance was not always easily enforced, but sometimes it led to religious intolerance and persecution (Elias, 2001).

Some areas exemplified religious tolerance through the existence of Muslims, Christians, and Jews living together harmoniously, sharing knowledge that enriched their respective cultures (Glick, 1999). This kind of tolerance often resulted from pragmatism as rulers recognised the advantages of diversity and cooperation (Meyer, 2006). In these cases, people could practice religion freely without being persecuted for it; hence, different religions coexisted peacefully (Baker, 2004).

However, religious intolerance could also manifest itself, leading to discrimination, expulsion, or violence against those of other faiths (Armstrong 2006). Religious conflicts, driven by political ambitions or ideological disparities, could lead to the suppression of minority religions and the imposition of religious uniformity (Smith 2011). Such intolerance may take the form of forced conversions, Inquisitions, or pogroms directed at religious minorities (MacCulloch 2011).

In general, the dynamics of religious tolerance and intolerance in medieval Europe were influenced by a complex interplay between political, social and cultural factors (Elias 2001). While there were instances of religious coexistence and cooperation, there were also periods of conflict and persecution based on religious differences. Knowledge about the intricacies of religious tolerance and intolerance is crucial for understanding Muslim-Christian-Jewish interactions in medieval Europe (Baker 2004).

Conversion and Apostasy

During the medieval period in Europe, conversion and apostasy were important topics in the religious landscape of that time (Horsley, 2012). Conversion is when a person changes his or her religion, usually from one faith to another. Different communities interacted with each other, and different religions spread throughout Europe, making this occurrence widespread (Elias, 2001).

On the other hand, apostasy meant renouncing one's faith, particularly for another religion or against organised religion as a whole (MacCulloch, 2011). This act was often controversial and could have severe social and legal consequences for those who chose to abandon their faith (Glick, 1999).

Both conversion and apostasy were influenced by various factors, such as social pressures, political motivations, and personal beliefs (Armstrong, 2006). The interactions between different religious communities in medieval Europe often led to debates and conflicts surrounding the issues of conversion and apostasy (Horsley, 2012).

The attitudes towards conversion and apostasy also differed from one religious group or region to another (Elias, 2001). There were societies that allowed for freedom of belief and were more tolerant of religious diversity, while others imposed severe penalties on those who converted or apostatised (Baker, 2004).

In general, the issues of conversion and apostasy are very important in understanding the religious dynamics of medieval Europe as well as the complexities of religious identity and practice during this period (Glick, 1999).

Religious Syncretism and Hybridity

During the medieval period, religious syncretism and hybridity were common themes in the interactions between different faiths (MacCulloch, 2011). As Islamic and Christian societies lived side by side, they naturally blended their religious practices and beliefs, resulting in a unique cultural and spiritual exchange (Elias, 2001).

One of the most important aspects of religious syncretism was borrowing from one religion to another (Horsley, 2012). For example, at places where there were intersections between Islamic and Christian communities, prayers, rituals, or even architectural styles often had an impact on each other (Glick, 1999). This led to a diverse landscape of religions where borders between them became indistinct, with people adopting customs from more than one tradition (Meyer, 2006).

Hybridity also played a significant role in shaping the religious landscape of medieval Europe (Armstrong, 2006). People who had both Islamic and Christian backgrounds, either due to mixed heritage or conversion, brought along a rich tapestry of beliefs and practices that combined elements from both faiths

(Baker, 2004). This amalgamation of traditions resulted in a distinct new spirituality, reflecting the complexity and diversity of the medieval world (MacCulloch, 2011).

Moreover, religious syncretism and hybridity were not limited to individual beliefs but also extended to religious institutions and structures (Elias, 2001). In some regions where religions interacted, churches and mosques displayed a mixture of architectural styles and decorative elements from Islamic and Christian traditions (Smith, 2011). This physical representation of syncretism was an example of how different faiths and cultures were interconnected (Glick, 1999).

In general, the phenomenon of religious syncretism and hybridity in medieval Europe highlights the fact that religion is dynamic and constantly changing (Meyer, 2006). By exchanging ideas, traditions, and cultural expressions with one another, communities underwent a process of mutual enrichment as well as transformation that shaped the spiritual landscape at this time (Armstrong, 2006).

Religious Institutions and Structures

Religious institutions and structures played a pivotal role in shaping the religious landscape of medieval Europe (MacCulloch, 2011). They were the focal points for power, influence, and fellowship among believers, providing a framework for religious practice and governance (Horsley, 2012). Religious institutions included a broad spectrum of organisations ranging from monasteries and convents to cathedral chapters and religious orders (Elias, 2001). These establishments often held sway over political and economic matters, thus controlling both spiritual and secular affairs (Baker, 2004).

Churches, cathedrals and mosques across Europe served as physical expressions of religious faith and devotion (Smith,

2011). These buildings were not only places of worship but also cultural centres where art was produced (Armstrong, 2006). The intricate architecture and decoration of these structures mirrored the religious beliefs and values of the communities that constructed them (Meyer, 2006). Religious institutions also had an important role in education and intellectual life; they functioned as centres of learning where monks lived or cathedral schools with scholars.

The hierarchy of religious institutions was often closely tied to the hierarchy of the broader society (Glick, 1999). Bishops, archbishops, and patriarchs who were at the top of the religious hierarchy had considerable spiritual and temporal authority (MacCulloch, 2011). Priests, monks, and nuns who administered sacraments and guided people spiritually also played a crucial role in this system (Elias, 2001). Religious orders such as Franciscans and Dominicans operated outside the traditional parish structure, focusing on specific missions or forms of worship (Baker, 2004).

Different regions and religious traditions had different ways of organising their religious institutions (Meyer, 2006). In some areas, bishops and abbots held political power along with spiritual authority, while in others, they were more independent, operating as centres for resistance against secular authorities (Horsley, 2012). However, despite these differences, religious institutions remained important aspects of medieval European religion, shaping the beliefs, practices, and identities of believers alike (MacCulloch, 2011).

Influence of Religious Leaders

Religious leaders in medieval Europe had a lot of power and influence over the beliefs and practices of their followers (Glick, 1999). These leaders included bishops, abbots, and priests, all of whom were very important in shaping the religious landscape at that time (MacCulloch, 2011). They were not only spiritual guides but also political figures who often wielded considerable authority (Horsley, 2012).

These religious leaders acted as intermediaries between God and people. They interpreted religious teachings and doctrines to the masses (Baker, 2004). They provided moral guidance, administered sacraments and oversaw worship practices within their communities (Elias, 2001). Their words and actions had the power to inspire and motivate their followers, thereby shaping their beliefs and behaviours (Smith, 2011).

Besides this, religious leaders often played a role in mediating conflicts and disputes within their communities. They used their moral authority to resolve disputes as well as maintain peace among them (Glick, 1999). Moreover, they worked towards promoting unity and cohesion among their followers by fostering a sense of belonging based on religious beliefs (Armstrong, 2006).

Also, religious leaders would often be involved in charitable works or assisting those who are vulnerable in society. By showing compassion through acts of service, they demonstrated the values of their faith, thus inspiring others to follow suit.

Their sphere of influence went beyond the spiritual, and they also had an impact on social norms and practices in their communities (Elias, 2001).

In general, religious leaders had a profound and extensive effect on medieval Europe (MacCulloch, 2011). Their teachings and activities played a crucial role in shaping the religious, social and political landscape of the era, thereby leaving indelible marks on the lives of their adherents (Smith, 2011).

Religious art and architecture, along with the societal and political shifts tied to religion, played an undeniably pivotal role in shaping medieval communities, particularly in Europe and the Islamic world. Here's a synthesis highlighting their impact, with a particular focus on the striking cultural and architectural achievements of the period:

Religious Art and Architecture in the Medieval World

Religious structures served as epicentres of devotion, culture, and power. They were not just functional spaces for worship but also bold manifestations of the artistic, theological, and social ideals of their creators.

Islamic Contributions

In Al-Andalus, the Great Mosque of Cordoba exemplifies the sophistication of Islamic architecture. Its horseshoe arches, mosaic-decorated mihrab, and a forest of columns reflect not only Islamic spirituality but also an innovative adaptation of local styles. Similarly, the Dome of the Rock in Jerusalem is a masterpiece that combines Byzantine and Islamic influences, encased in geometric patterns and inscriptions from the Qur'an. These structures illustrate the beauty of Islamic calligraphy, symmetry, and ornamentation while signalling the dominance and permanence of Islamic civilisation during their construction.

Beyond their religious roles, these buildings symbolised the prestige and authority of rulers who commissioned them. They also blended cultures: in Al-Andalus, for instance, Islamic art absorbed elements of Roman masonry and Visigothic traditions, creating a visually harmonious yet distinct new style.

Christian Achievements

In Christian Europe, Notre Dame in Paris, with its soaring Gothic buttresses and exquisite stained-glass windows, and St. Peter's Basilica in Rome, a pinnacle of Renaissance grandeur, stand as monumental achievements of devotion and artistic ingenuity. These cathedrals reflected the divine aspirations of medieval Christianity through their verticality, reaching towards the heavens as expressions of faith. The intricate depictions of biblical scenes in sculptures and glass informed an often largely illiterate populace about theological narratives, fostering a shared spiritual culture.

Christian art expanded beyond architecture, dominating media like illuminated manuscripts and religious sculptures. These carvings and paintings were not merely decoration—they were pedagogical and devotional tools that gave believers access to Christian mysteries and promoted religious orthodoxy.

The Societal and Political Ramifications of Religion

Religious shifts and institutions profoundly shaped medieval societies, transcending the sphere of belief to influence governance, economics, and inter-communal relationships.

Power Dynamics and Governance

In Christian Europe, the Catholic Church became a political powerhouse. Monarchs allied with or were subject to ecclesiastical authorities, with doctrines like the divine right of kings tying secular rule to God's will. The Church's influence extended to shaping laws, diplomacy, and education.

In the Islamic world, rulers embraced and enforced religious governance with laws underpinned by Islamic jurisprudence (Sharia). In Al-Andalus, Islam not only shaped governance but also enabled the promotion of interfaith tolerance under the dhimmi system, allowing Christians and Jews certain freedoms while maintaining Islamic primacy.

Religious Identity and Social Structure

Religious identity was critical to socio-economic mobility. In regions under Islamic rule, conversion to Islam often offered greater access to privileges and opportunities. Some non-Muslim communities adapted to preserve their status, contributing to the syncretism that enriched Islamic Spain's culture. Conversely, in Christian territories, adopting Christianity (or being Catholic as opposed to heretical sects) could similarly elevate one's social rank.

Interfaith interactions, particularly in multi-religious societies like Al-Andalus, led to cultural exchange, visible in everything from philosophy to cuisine. Architecture also reflected these dynamics; for example, Gothic chapels bore structural influences borrowed from Islamic engineering techniques, while mosques and palaces drew on designs seen in Roman and Visigothic structures.

Religious Structures as Political Symbols

Religious buildings often represented a ruler's claim to authority and their transcendent connection to a divine mandate. The Great Mosque of Cordoba showcased the Umayyad Caliphate's wealth and sophistication, while Notre Dame underscored the consolidation of Paris as a centre of Christian rule. These monumental projects projected power domestically and demonstrated civilisation's greatness to rival cultures.

Legacy

The artistic, social, and political changes tied to religion during this period left a lasting legacy. Through architecture, the synthesis of religious and cultural ideals lives on—whether in the dazzling muqarnas vaulting of Islamic palaces or the rose windows of Gothic cathedrals.

These achievements provide modern observers with a tangible link to medieval societies' spiritual and political aspirations while reminding us of how shared human creativity transcended religious boundaries to produce enduring beauty.

Chapter 12

Military Strategies and Tactics

INTRODUCTION TO MILITARY STRATEGIES

Warfare, an intricate and continuously transforming domain, demands a delicate balance of calculated strategy, proactive tactics, and insightful leadership. The backbone of any triumphant campaign lies in its military strategies, which orchestrate movements, direct combat patterns, and ultimately decide the outcomes of armed conflicts. During the Islamic conquests in Europe, these strategies proved pivotal, enabling the expansion of Islamic dominion and establishing robust governance in newly acquired territories. Within this context, we will uncover the sophisticated approaches, groundbreaking innovations, and steadfast leadership that fuelled the Islamic forces' success, shedding light on how these elements defined one of history's most transformative periods.

THE ROLE OF LEADERSHIP IN WARFARE

Leadership, often the decisive factor in moments of chaotic conflict, became the linchpin of the Islamic conquests. Commanders not only shaped battlefield outcomes through their decisions but also forged the spirit and discipline of their troops. Without strong leadership readily adapting to the unpredictability of warfare, victories would have been far more elusive. Military leadership demanded a multifaceted skill set—insight into enemy vulnerabilities, mastery over varied terrains, and a thorough grasp of their own soldiers' capabilities. Alongside these analytical abilities was an equally indispensable skill: the art of rallying, inspiring, and invigorating warriors. Battlefield conditions required rapid decision-making, frequently under pressure, while facing unforeseen challenges. Military leaders had to strike a balance between meticulous planning and flexible improvisation. The hallmark of these commanders was their bravery—not from the safety of the rear lines but through leading by example on the front lines. Standing shoulder to shoulder with their troops, they embodied courage, resilience, and unwavering determination. This kind of leadership fostered loyalty that could not be matched by sheer commands alone. The sense of camaraderie built between leaders and soldiers forged armies capable of enduring even the most gruelling battles (Antczak et al., 2024).

Communication also stood as a keystone of effective military leadership. Commanders needed to articulate strategies with precision, leaving no room for ambiguity. On the battlefield, where unexpected shifts could redefine the fight in moments, clarity ensured cohesion. A well-delivered directive could transform potential chaos into synchronised action, especially during manoeuvres like flanking or counterattacking. Perhaps equally critical was adaptability—a quality separating competent leaders from extraordinary ones. In the ever-shifting sands of war, no plan survived unchanged in combat. Adaptable commanders redefined their tactics mid-engagement, turning perceived disadvantages into tactical opportunities. Such skill in the exploitation of weaknesses—whether a lapse in enemy defences or underutilised geographical features—exemplified the ingenuity required for victory. Leadership during the Islamic conquests acted as the cornerstone beneath every tactical advantage. With strategic foresight, exemplary bravery, and the flexibility to pivot when necessary, these leaders orchestrated campaigns that shaped the trajectory of an entire era.

THE SYNERGY OF CAVALRY AND INFANTRY

When it came to assembling versatile and effective armies, the Islamic forces mastered the art of combining cavalry and infantry into a single, cohesive military machine (Anderson et al., 2023). Each branch, despite its unique role, formed a symbiotic relationship with the other, resulting in unparalleled battlefield supremacy. The cavalry, steered by dynamic horsemen, brought speed and unpredictability into the theatre of war. Striking suddenly and manoeuvring out just as swiftly, this mounted force excelled at disruption tactics—fracturing enemy formations and compelling them to scatter (Comstock et al., 2023). Their penchant for hit-and-run methods and their proficiency in reconnaissance made them an invaluable asset for outmanoeuvring opponents. In instances requiring bold moves, they executed sweeping flanking operations with unrelenting precision.

On the other hand, infantry forces provided the foundation upon which battles were sustained. These foot soldiers endured the weight of prolonged engagements with singular determination. Armed with weapons such as swords, spears, and shields, infantry units excelled in both offence and defence. They held their ground in sieges, pressed forward during assaults, and ensured control over newly seized territories. The infantry's resilience balanced the cavalry's fluid mobility, grounding the army and ensuring durability in drawn-out conflicts. What made this combination flourish, however, was more than the individual strengths of cavalry or infantry—it was their collaboration. Cavalry softened enemy lines with their swift and destabilising attacks, creating openings that infantry could forcefully exploit. Conversely, while infantry anchored the battlefield, cavalry shielded their flanks, offering protection and ensuring free movement. The seamless interplay between mobility and endurance gave Islamic armies the adaptability to tackle a variety of challenges, from open-field skirmishes to lengthy sieges. This dynamic combination became a defining feature of Islamic military operations. The synergy between the cavalry's ample speed and agility, alongside the infantry's unwavering grit and steadfastness, enabled commanders to mount strategic offensives and maintain a versatile edge in their campaigns across Europe (Anderson et al., 2023).

THE ART OF SIEGE WARFARE: A CALCULATED SYMPHONY OF STRATEGY AND INGENUITY

Siege warfare during the Islamic conquests of Europe was far more than a clash of brute force; it was an intricate dance of patience, engineering brilliance, and psychological mastery. Each besieged stronghold presented a formidable challenge—not simply as physical barriers of stone but as proud emblems of resistance. To overcome these defences, Muslim armies devised methods that thrived on outthinking, outrunning, and ultimately outlasting their opponents (Sikandar Shah, 2023). Siege engines, such as trebuchets and mangonels, sat at the forefront of these calculated assaults. These colossal weapons, built for ruin, could launch masonry-shattering projectiles or fiery payloads with chilling precision. A city's walls, once towering declarations of invincibility, were laid bare to the relentless impact of these machines. More than tools of destruction, they were instruments of fear—a reminder to defenders that every barricade had its breaking point. However, applying raw power alone was rarely the avenue to victory. It was the subtle, less visible approaches that often wreaked the greatest havoc (Sikandar Shah, 2023). From beneath the earth, armies deployed sappers and mining engineers in a deadly game of subversion. By tunnelling under walls and setting strategic explosives or timber fires, they sought to unbalance not just the fortifications but the fragile confidence of defenders. A city's powerful walls, symbols of its permanence, could collapse without warning—turning what was once steadfast into a heap of despairing rubble. This duality of direct force and quiet sabotage embodied the essence of Islamic siege strategy: a union of patience and precision.

Yet the battlefield of the mind was often where the decisive blows were struck. Muslim forces honed psychological warfare to a grim art. Disease was weaponised as a ghastly messenger, with plague-ridden corpses hurled over city ramparts, spreading pestilence and eroding both morale and population. Rumoured reinforcements or exaggerated depictions of invincible war machines were whispered into enemy ears, sowing doubt as effectively as any battering ram could crush stone. Defenders, starved of stability and unity, often capitulated before a final blow was ever struck. None of these tactics thrived in isolation. Siege operations demanded logistical cunning on an extraordinary scale. Armies laying siege had to endure long campaigns, ensuring steady supplies while watching for escapees or relief forces seeking to break their encirclement (Scott Pribble, 2023). A commander's ability to balance forceful assault with biding patience determined whether a campaign would falter or flourish. Those who could adapt displayed artistry in leadership, uniting inventive technology, military discipline, and a chess master's foresight. For Muslim leaders, the fall of cities once deemed untouchable wasn't merely a military achievement; it was a deliberate reshaping of political and cultural landscapes. Each siege carried the weight of territorial conquest and the legacy of strategic ingenuity. By weaving together tactical flexibility, psychological mastery, and unrelenting dedication, Islamic armies set a precedent for siege warfare—teetering between calculated destruction and the finesse of innovation.

MARITIME DOMINANCE: THE PULSE OF NAVAL WARFARE IN ISLAMIC CONQUESTS

The conquest of lands often begins not on soil but upon the vast, shifting seas. For Islamic forces during their European campaigns, naval warfare became an indispensable pillar of their strategy, granting them the agility to disrupt enemy lines, control maritime arteries, and extend influence far beyond the horizon. The Mediterranean and its surrounding waters transformed into theatres of both unrelenting battles and subtle manoeuvres. At the heart of Islamic naval dominance was a mastery of shipbuilding and naval innovation. Swift, manoeuvrable vessels armed with advanced weaponry like the terrifying Greek fire—a flammable substance capable of igniting even upon water—became the cornerstone of their fleets. These ships thrived in any operation: devastating enemy flotillas in sea skirmishes, intercepting supply lines, or executing coastal bombardments that softened enemy fortresses before the main assault arrived (Cropsey et al., 2023). Their speed and adaptability turned the seas into highways of opportunity. The unity of land and sea forces added a lethal versatility to Islamic campaigns. Amphibious operations blurred the boundary between naval and terrestrial warfare. Fleets accompanied invading armies, targeting vulnerable coastal strongholds or cutting enemy reinforcements at their source. This synchronised approach ensured that even the most fortified cities were left isolated and vulnerable.

However, raw combat prowess was merely one thread in the tapestry of naval superiority. Equally crucial was intelligence. Islamic fleets, adept at reconnaissance, patrolled key routes not only to intercept ships but also to study the rhythms of enemy movements. Each wave or whisper of enemy activity became a strand of vital information woven into an ever-changing plan that outpaced their adversaries ('Brill', 2022). More than expansion and conquest, maritime supremacy demonstrated how control of the seas could dictate the fortunes of nations. Islamic forces understood that naval warfare was not a separate domain of conflict but a vital organ within the body of war itself—a force that dictated trade, reinforcements, and territorial reach. By weaving together technological ingenuity, tactical foresight, and relentless adaptability, they redefined the role of naval power in medieval military strategy. Through both their naval conquests and siege campaigns, Islamic forces showed an unparalleled ability to adapt to a variety of battlefronts. From the relentless battering of fortress walls to the swift dominance of open seas, their military acumen set them apart as a force to be reckoned with, not just in Europe but across the medieval world.

INTELLIGENCE GATHERING AND ESPIONAGE

Intelligence gathering and espionage were pivotal in driving the success of the Islamic conquests in Europe, laying the groundwork for many military triumphs. Islamic commanders relied heavily on spies who operated deep within enemy territories, often disguised as merchants, pilgrims, artisans, or traders. This allowed them to blend seamlessly into local populations while acquiring intelligence on enemy troop movements, resource lines, fortifications, and potential vulnerabilities. These covert missions often shaped the strategic decisions made by commanders, giving them the foresight to exploit enemy weaknesses.

A key facet of espionage during this time was the interception and decryption of enemy communications. Islamic cryptanalysts used advanced skills in mathematics and linguistic analysis to break codes and cyphers, revealing enemy plans and strategies (Hoskins et al., 2024). This art of cryptology not only gave the Islamic forces a tactical advantage but also played a psychological role, as enemies were sometimes unaware that their secret communications had been compromised. The ability to intercept battlefield messages or logistic orders ensured that Islamic forces could preempt enemy moves and disrupt supply chains effectively. Disguise and deception were vital elements of espionage. Spies often used misinformation to sow discord within enemy ranks or feign allegiance to weaken morale (Achu et al., 2022). Collaborative spy networks—often run by skilled handlers—used secret codes, hidden couriers, and inconspicuous signals to transfer invaluable intelligence without compromising operations. Spycraft of this period reflects a sophisticated understanding of both human psychology and warfare logistics, making it a cornerstone of the Islamic conquest strategy.

DEFENSIVE FORTIFICATIONS AND STRONGHOLDS

Defensive fortifications were a central element of both strategic offensives and territorial consolidation during the Islamic conquests in Europe. The building and maintenance of strongholds, fortified cities, and castles formed the backbone of Islamic efforts to maintain control over contested territories (Mabelitini et al., 2024). These fortifications were often positioned at critical locations—river crossings, trade routes, and mountain passes—allowing forces to impede the advance of enemy armies or secure access to vital resources. Islamic engineers and architects contributed significantly to fortification design, inspired by diverse influences, from Byzantine structures to complex Persian fortresses (Bruso et al., 2022). Conquered cities such as Toledo and Zaragoza were often retrofitted with reinforced walls, moats, and towers, transforming them into resilient defensive hubs.

Islamic strongholds were multipurpose—they provided a secure base where supplies, weapons, and troops could be stored while also functioning as centres of governance, cementing control over newly acquired regions. On the offensive side, Islamic armies frequently encountered highly fortified cities and castles. To breach these, they implemented innovative measures in siege warfare. Engines of war, including mangonels, trebuchets, and battering rams, were employed to weaken walls and penetrate gates. Siege towers and tunnels (sappers) enabled ground forces to bypass external fortifications, while psychological tactics—such as blockades to cut off food and water supplies—compounded the pressure on defenders. The flexibility and efficiency of these tactics ensured that even the most formidable defensive structures could eventually be subdued. Ultimately, the careful balance between fortification construction and the ability to dismantle enemy strongholds contributed significantly to the durability of Islamic conquests, protecting territories from counterattacks while expanding their military and political reach.

USE OF MILITARY TECHNOLOGY AND INNOVATION

The Islamic conquests in Europe were underpinned by the strategic use of advanced military technology and the integration of innovative tactics, both of which granted Muslim forces a marked edge in combat. The adaptability and ingenuity of the Islamic armies allowed them to co-opt, refine, and deploy technologies drawn from a wide array of cultures, from the Byzantine Empire to the Sassanian Persians. Islamic forces excelled in the development and use of siege weaponry. Machines like trebuchets and mangonels are capable of hurling projectiles with incredible precision, but they have weakened enemy fortifications with relentless bombardment. Battering rams, augmented by protective covers, allowed soldiers to reach fortified gates under the cover of fire. Excavation techniques for tunnelling beneath enemy walls—sometimes with explosives or collapsible timber supports—demonstrated their technical expertise in siegecraft. This gave commanders an unparalleled ability to dismantle even the most robust defensive structures.

One of the most distinctive technological advancements was the use of Greek Fire, an incendiary compound deployed primarily in naval warfare. Fired through pressurised siphons or hurled in clay pots, the substance was nearly impossible to extinguish and created chaos among enemy fleets, particularly in maritime sieges and battles (Crenshaw et al., 2023). Greek Fire was instrumental in securing key waterways and ports, crucial for both trade and military dominance. Beyond siege technology, Islamic forces utilised sophisticated weaponry and armour that elevated their infantry and cavalry. The use of composite bows—smaller yet far more powerful than traditional wooden bows—gave archers increased range and impact. Scimitars, with their curved design, were highly effective in close combat, offering speed and manoeuvrability. Soldiers were often equipped with advanced chainmail and layered shields, improving both protection and mobility. Horse-mounted warriors combined shock tactics with precision, using lances and swords in tightly coordinated cavalry charges. Tactical innovation amplified the effectiveness of this technological edge. Feigned retreats—a strategy intended to lure enemies into ambushes—proved devastatingly effective against less disciplined opponents. The coordination of light and heavy cavalry, combined with skirmish tactics by archers, allowed for strategic flexibility even in the face of numerically superior enemies. The Islamic armies' ability to integrate groundbreaking technologies and innovative strategies into cohesive operations exemplified their military prowess (Crenshaw et al., 2023). These advancements not only facilitated battlefield successes but also ensured the long-term consolidation of their territorial gains in Europe.

LOGISTICS AND SUPPLY CHAIN MANAGEMENT DURING THE ISLAMIC CONQUESTS

The effectiveness of the Islamic conquests in Europe relied heavily on robust logistics and meticulous supply chain management. The armies often operated far from their home base, through uncharted and challenging terrains, necessitating a well-coordinated system to sustain prolonged campaigns. The logistical framework ensured the steady movement of troops, equipment, and provisions across vast distances (Haines et al., 2022). Supply caravans consisting of pack animals, carts, and boats formed the backbone of this system, facilitating the transport of essentials such as food, water, weapons, and medical supplies. Key to this strategy was the establishment of supply depots and waystations positioned at strategic intervals along campaign routes. These hubs stockpiled resources to resupply advancing forces, reducing reliance on vulnerable long-distance supply lines.

Communication was another pivotal component. A network of couriers and messengers ensured the timely exchange of orders, maps, and intelligence reports between commanders and the frontline. This allowed leaders to remain responsive to the rapid pace of military operations, adjusting strategies based on fresh information. The speed and efficiency of this communication framework were critical in directing reinforcements or redirecting resources where needed (Matar et al., 2023). Weaponry and equipment maintenance also received considerable attention. Mobile workshops and armouries were integral to campaigns, where skilled craftsmen repaired damaged tools of war or manufactured replacements on-site. This ensured soldiers remained well-equipped despite the inevitable wear and tear of extended engagements. Moreover, logistics extended beyond physical supplies to include the organisation of medical services. Field hospitals were mobilised to treat wounded fighters and staffed by physicians and surgeons with access to medical supplies. This care not only preserved manpower but also bolstered the morale of troops, who knew their wellbeing was prioritised. Ultimately, the Islamic forces' logistical acumen was a cornerstone of their military success. Through precise planning, resource allocation, and efficient communication, they overcame the challenges of sustaining large armies across varied and often hostile terrains.

ADAPTATION TO VARIED BATTLEFIELDS

The diverse geography of Europe during the Islamic conquests dictated a need for adaptability on the battlefield. From rugged mountain ranges and dense forests to expansive plains and fortified cities, the ability to tailor tactics to the environment became a hallmark of their military strategy. This complexity mirrors the strategic orchestration seen in modern contexts, such as Ukraine's digital and psychological warfare tactics, which also require similar adaptability to multifaceted environments (Brittain-Hale et al., 2023). Furthermore, understanding the historical context of military adaptation, as seen in the establishment of the K9 Corps during World War II, highlights the long-standing necessity for military forces to evolve their strategies according to the challenges presented by diverse terrains (Phillips et al., 2023).

A. Mountain Warfare

In the highland territories, such as the Pyrenees or the Balkan mountain ranges, traditional large-scale manoeuvres were constrained. Islamic forces employed guerrilla tactics to offset these difficulties. By mastering ambushes and hit-and-run warfare, they disrupted enemy supply lines and weakened opposition forces without engaging in direct confrontation (Aima Tahir et al., 2023). Knowledge of local terrain, often aided by scouts or allied tribes, proved invaluable for navigating passes and establishing defensible positions (Osflaten et al., 2023).

B. Plains Combat

Conversely, on open flatlands like the Hungarian or Southern French plains, the Islamic armies capitalised on the mobility of their cavalry. With light, highly manoeuvrable horsemen, they executed swift and decisive strikes, often attacking flanks or encircling adversaries before retreating. Utilising their mastery of coordinated cavalry manoeuvres, they gained the upper hand by exploiting the open terrain to maximise their speed and military precision (Choudhury et al., 2023). This approach reflects broader military strategies where terrain plays a crucial role in operational effectiveness, similar to the tactical principles observed during the American Civil War, where commanders navigated geographical features to enhance their strategic options (Pezzati et al., 2024).

C. Forest Warfare

Dense forests, like those of the Ardennes or Black Forest, presented a distinct challenge due to restricted visibility and mobility. Here, the forces adopted compact, flexible formations to navigate the underbrush (DAR et al., 2022). Soldiers employed stealth and ambush tactics to neutralise opposing troops, functioning within the framework of total war concepts that emphasise mobilising all available resources and unconventional tactics (Ekah Robert Ekah, 2022). The natural cover provided by forested regions became an asset for surprise attacks, allowing smaller units to overcome numerically superior foes.

D. Siege Warfare in Urban Environments

In confronting fortified urban centres such as Toledo or Constantinople, the Islamic forces demonstrated exceptional siegecraft. They employed siege engines, including catapults, battering rams, and towers, to breach defensive walls (Cunha et al., 2024). Tunnel digging, or sapping, further weakened fortifications, while psychological tactics—such as cutting off supplies or spreading fear—undermined defenders' resilience. This approach reflects the changing character of urban operations, where the complexities of human settlement and interactions add layers of challenge to military endeavours (Cunha et al., 2024). Patience and ingenuity were pivotal, as the Islamic armies paired traditional siege techniques with methods tailored to the specific challenges of each city.

Chapter 13

Legacy and Memory

Reflections on the Islamic Conquests in Europe

The Islamic conquests across Europe have etched a profound legacy, one that continues to ripple through the continent's history and consciousness. These events, preserved in chronicles, enduring landmarks, and artistic achievements, reveal layers of cultural interaction that have shaped European identity in multifaceted ways. They serve as a reminder not just of conquest but of adaptation, exchange, and the intricate intertwining of civilisations that define Europe's complex tapestry. Through such recollection, one glimpses a dance of histories—where the Islamic and European worlds intersected, influenced and transformed one another across the centuries.

Transformative Impact on European Societies

The influence of the Islamic conquests reverberated like an echo through time, touching countless aspects of European life. These encounters catalysed transformations at both societal and intellectual levels, profoundly altering the continent's course. Yet, it wasn't merely battles and boundaries that left their mark; an unparalleled exchange of knowledge flowed through this interconnection, forever embedding itself in Europe's cultural DNA.

Intriguingly, the introduction of Islamic scientific thought, philosophy, and literary treasures initiated an intellectual flourishing that reshaped Europe's intellectual landscape. Astronomy, medicine, and mathematics were suddenly revitalised by ideas from Islamic scholars like Al-Khwarizmi and Avicenna, whose manuscripts sparkled like embers in the dim corridors of medieval Europe. These illuminations eventually ignited the fires of the Renaissance and, later, the Scientific Revolution, two pivotal epochs in European history.

But this impact extended beyond scholarly pursuits. The arrival of Muslim populations in regions like Andalucía and Sicily nurtured dynamic, multicultural societies. Here, Christians, Jews, and Muslims coexisted—periodically in tension, yet persistently in dialogue. This blending of communities fostered a spirit of cultural exchange, evident in the social norms that accommodated diversity, tolerance, and mutual respect. Such pluralistic undercurrents, though at times fraught with conflict, planted enduring seeds for a more interconnected European society.

The Threads of Art, Architecture, and Daily Life

Where knowledge flowed, so, too, did artistry bloom. The architectural legacy of the Islamic conquests is often hailed as one of the most visible markers of this confluence. Structures like the Alhambra in Granada stand as awe-inspiring testaments to the sophistication of Islamic design, its geometric elegance resonating with divine symbolism. Arches and domes, once novel to many European eyes, began adorning cathedrals and palaces, reshaping Europe's architectural vocabulary. Meanwhile, intricate mosaics and dazzling tilework reflected not just artistry but a profound aesthetic philosophy rooted in unity and balance.

The influence spilt into more intimate corners of daily life as culinary traditions diversified across borders. Vibrant spices, exotic ingredients, and innovative cooking techniques infused medieval European kitchens, gradually transforming local cuisines into a fusion of flavours. These sensory exchanges weren't limited to food—music and literature, too, bore the marks of shared creativity, with instruments like the oud influencing the evolution of European stringed instruments and poetic traditions borrowing from Arabic lyrical forms.

A Lingering Legacy

To view the Islamic conquests purely through the lens of military campaigns is to miss their true, enduring significance. Beyond the dust of battlefields, they left behind bridges of culture, knowledge, and creativity that continue to shape modern European identity. The legacy is a vibrant tapestry of learning, artistry, and adaptability, a testament to the richness inherent in cross-cultural exchange. The resonance of this past speaks clearly to the potential of interconnectedness—not as a footnote of history but as a guide for the present.

Through the lens of this legacy, one can appreciate Europe not as a singular narrative but as a mosaic—where diversity is not merely an inevitability of geography but a strength drawn from centuries of shared human endeavour. The memory of these conquests lives on, not only in stone and script but in the very fabric of Europe itself, reminding us of the dynamism that lies at the heart of historical transformation.

Historical Narratives and Memory

The collective memory of the Islamic conquests in Europe has been deeply marked by their impact on Islamic as well as European societies (Hodgson, 1974). These narratives have been retold over time to change how they are remembered and understood (Esposito, 1999). The memory of these conquests reminds us of the complex interactions between different cultures and civilisations during this period (McCormick, 2001).

Islamic histories often celebrate the conquests as major achievements that expanded the influence of the Islamic caliphate and brought new lands under Muslim rule (Eisenberg, 2005). They emphasise the courage and military might of the Islamic armies as well as the successful spread of Islam's culture and values in newly conquered areas (Glick, 2005). The conquests are depicted as a manifestation of divine will and an indication of the strength of Islamic civilisation (Hodgson, 1974).

Islamic conquests in European histories are often seen through a different prism, which highlights the conflicts and tensions that resulted from these invasions (Esposito, 1999). The memory of these conquests is sometimes shaded with feelings of bitterness and fear towards the so-called "Other." Islamic conquerors are often depicted as invaders who threatened the stability and security of Christian Europe in European narratives (McCormick, 2001). These stories serve to reinforce ideas of Christian identity and the need to defend against outside threats (Hodgson, 1974).

However, historical accounts of Islamic conquests have a significant impact on our understanding of this period. They provide valuable insights into the intricate power dynamics, cultural differences, and religious aspects that define interactions between Islamic and European societies (Eisenberg, 2005). By examining these narratives and reflecting on their construction and remembrance, we can develop a better appreciation for the legacy of Islamic conquests in Europe that still influences our world today (Glick, 2005).

Religious Legacy and Interactions

The Islamic conquests of Europe were significantly influenced by religious beliefs and practices, which affected interactions between different religions and left a long-lasting legacy in the region (McNeill, 1992). The advent of Islamic rulers resulted in a complex intermingling of religious traditions that led to a period of coexistence, conflict, and cultural interchange (Esposito, 1999).

Islamic leaders often practised religious tolerance policies that allowed Christians and Jews to worship within their territories (Glick, 2005). This approach promoted a varied religious landscape and enabled harmonious relationships among various religious communities (Eisenberg, 2005). In some instances, even non-Muslim officials and advisers were employed by Islamic rulers, demonstrating an unusual level of pluralistic religion in medieval Europe (Hodgson, 1974).

Muslims' conquests triggered intellectual and theological exchanges between Muslim scholars on the one hand and Christian or Jewish scholars on the other. Translation projects were launched to translate works from Greek, Latin, Arabic, and Hebrew, leading to the preservation and spread of knowledge across religious lines (Glick, 2005). These cultural exchanges shaped science, philosophy, and literature in medieval Europe, thus creating a rich intellectual tradition that went beyond religious divisions (Esposito, 1999).

Islamic rulers often influenced religious institutions and practices (Eisenberg, 2005). European landscapes were marked by Islamic architecture and art styles that blended with existing traditions to create a unique fusion of artistic expression (Glick, 2005). Similarly, the Islamic conquests introduced new religious practices and rituals that influenced local customs and traditions, highlighting the interconnectedness of religious beliefs and cultural practices (Hodgson, 1974).

In general, the religious legacy of the Islamic conquests in Europe demonstrates how complex interactions between different faiths have had lasting effects on religious, cultural, and intellectual developments in this region (McCormick, 2001).

Artistic and Literary Contributions

During the Islamic conquests in Europe, artistic and literary contributions significantly shaped the cultural landscape of the region (Esposito, 1999). For centuries, European art and literature were influenced by new styles, techniques, and perspectives from Islamic artists and writers (Glick, 2005). A vibrant exchange of cultures was created through a combination of European artistic traditions with those from Islam, resulting in a richly diverse society for both parties involved (Eisenberg, 2005).

Islamic calligraphy, geometric patterns, and complex designs found their way into European art, architecture, and manuscripts, leaving a lasting impact on the continent's visual culture (McCormick, 2001). Literary works from the Islamic world inspired European writers to explore new themes, storytelling techniques, and perspectives, leading to the development of a rich literary tradition that drew from both Islamic and European sources (Esposito, 1999). The artistic and literary contributions of the Islamic conquests continue to be celebrated and studied today for their role in shaping the cultural heritage of Europe (Glick, 2005).

Legends and Myths Surrounding the Conquests

Legends and myths have long been intertwined with the Islamic conquests in Europe, shaping popular perceptions and historical narratives (Hodgson, 1974). These myths often reflect the fears and anxieties of the conquered peoples, portraying Muslim invaders as merciless and barbaric (Eisenberg, 2005). Tales of heroic resistance abound with miraculous interventions, which highlight struggles between Christian defenders and Islamic conquerors (McCormick, 2001).

The story of Roland, the hero of the Battle of Roncevaux Pass, is one of the most enduring myths (Hodgson, 1974). The epic poem "The Song of Roland" tells us that Roland fought bravely against the forces of Muslims led by the Emir of Cordoba and even died to protect Charlemagne's retreating army. This tale has been immortalised in art and literature as a symbol of Christianity's defence against Islam (Eisenberg, 2005).

El Cid is another well-known myth; he was a noble knight who fought both for and against Muslim rulers in Spain (Glick, 2005). His feats have been celebrated in countless poems and ballads, which portray him as a fearless defender of Christian principles in an Islamic-dominated Iberian Peninsula (McCormick, 2001).

However much these myths are popularly held, historians warn that they should not be taken at face value. Many were distorted over time to suit political or ideological ends, thereby obscuring the intricate realities surrounding Islamic conquests (Hodgson, 1974). By peeling back layers of legend and myth, we can gain better insight into the historical dynamics at work during this turbulent period in European history (Eisenberg, 2005).

The impact of these myths and legends is still felt in present-day discussions about the Islamic conquests in Europe (Esposito, 1999). To some people, they are considered stories that warn against religious conflicts and cultural clashes; to others, they are seen as symbols of endurance and resistance against challenges (Glick, 2005). In any case, they remind us that myths and legends have a way of shaping our historical understanding.

Commemoration and Memorials

McCormick (2001) states that commemoration and memorials are important in preserving the memory of Islamic conquests in Europe. Numerous monuments, plaques, and museums across the continent are dedicated to honouring these events and individuals (Esposito, 1999). These physical reminders stand as a testament to the lasting impact of conquests and the diverse cultural exchange that took place (Glick, 2005).

One of the most well-known memorials is Alhambra in Granada, Spain (Eisenberg, 2005). This beautiful fortress and palace complex was built by the Nasrid dynasty to represent Islamic rule in Spain. Its intricate architecture, lush gardens, and detailed tilework pay homage to the rich artistic heritage left behind by Islam's rulership (McCormick, 2001).

Aside from physical monuments, commemorative events are held throughout Europe to honour Islamic conquests (Glick, 2005). Such events often include lectures, exhibitions, or performances designed to highlight the cultural and historical importance of this period.

Moreover, academic research and scholarship also preserve the legacy of Islamic invasions in Europe. Historians, archaeologists, and cultural experts continue to study and interpret the effects of these invasions on European societies, thus ensuring that this period remains present and meaningful (Eisenberg, 2005).

As we move forward into the future, it is important to remember and pay tribute to the legacy of Islamic invasions in Europe (McCormick, 2001). By preserving and celebrating this history, we can gain a better understanding of the intricate interactions and exchanges that have shaped our world today (Glick, 2005).

Legacy in Contemporary Europe

The legacy of Islamic invasions in Europe still shapes modern times (Hodgson, 1974). From architecture and art, which are still influenced by it, to cultural exchanges that shaped European societies, the influence of this period is still felt (Esposito, 1999). Modern Europe stands as a testament to the complicated interplay between different civilisations as well as the long-lasting consequences of historical conquests (Eisenberg, 2005).

Islamic architecture and design in European cities still remind people of the cross-cultural exchange that occurred years ago (Glick, 2005). The fusion of Islamic and European styles has resulted in a unique aesthetic that is celebrated and preserved to this day. This is evident in the complex patterns of Andalusian palaces and the tall minarets seen on city skylines, which testify to the legacy of Islamic rule in Europe's urban fabric (Eisenberg, 2005).

Apart from this, there are many other aspects that remain as a result of Islamic conquests in European societies, such as religious practices, languages, and social customs (McCormick, 2001). The combination of Islamic and Christian traditions led to new forms of art, literature, and music, which continue to be sources of inspiration for creativity and innovation (Esposito, 1999). In fact, it was through interactions between different civilisations during this period that European culture became so diverse and rich (Glick, 2005).

Moreover, contemporary narratives and historical accounts are still influenced by memories of these conquests (Hodgson, 1974). Scholars and historians have continued to study them, thereby revealing their complexities. Therefore, revisiting history helps us to better understand our present as well as appreciate how interconnected world history is (Eisenberg, 2005).

In conclusion, the legacy of Islamic conquests in Europe goes beyond time itself. It is a constant reminder of the power of cultural intermingling and the transformational consequences of historical events (Esposito, 1999). By exploring and preserving this heritage, we ensure that future generations can learn from the past and continue to celebrate European diversity (Glick, 2005).

Lessons for Future Generations

It is evident that there are important lessons for future generations as we reflect on the heritage left behind by Islamic conquests in Europe (Hodgson, 1974). The complex interactions and exchanges that took place during this period serve as a reminder of how crucial cultural diversity and intercultural dialogue are (Glick, 2005). By studying the impacts of these conquests, we can understand how different civilisations can coexist positively with each other (Esposito, 1999).

One of the most important things I learned is the importance of tolerance and acceptance towards different religious and cultural traditions (Eisenberg, 2005). This history of Islamic conquests in Europe reveals how embracing diversity and promoting a climate of mutual respect and understanding can be beneficial. By learning from our past, we can work towards creating more inclusive societies that recognise the value of diverse cultural heritages (Glick, 2005).

In addition, the economic and trade networks which emerged as a result of Islamic conquests show how powerful cross-cultural collaboration and exchange could be (McCormick, 2001). These historical examples can help future generations make efforts to create more integrated global economies that are mutually beneficial to all involved parties (Esposito, 1999). Cooperation across borders will lead to prosperity for all nations across the globe (Hodgson, 1974).

Moreover, military strategies and tactics employed during Islamic conquests reveal the significance of adaptability and innovation in changing situations (Eisenberg, 2005). The leaders during this time period showed resourcefulness and strategic thinking, from which future generations can draw inspiration by adjusting their approaches to new challenges or opportunities (Glick, 2005).

In general, the legacy of Islamic conquest in Europe is a reminder of the intricacies of history and how past events still affect our societies today (Esposito, 1999). The future generations can be better placed to face the challenges and opportunities that come with living in an increasingly interconnected world by studying this period with an open mind and a willingness to learn from the past (McCormick, 2001).

Chapter 14

Summary of key findings

Context: Giving an overview of the research focus and methodologies used to provide a background for the key findings

Islamic conquests in Europe began in the early 7th century and constituted a significant era of change and interaction between different civilisations. These conquests had far-reaching effects on Europe, including redefining political boundaries, cultural practices, and religious beliefs.

This section's research focus is on providing a nuanced understanding of the motivations behind Islamic conquests in Europe and the methodologies used to study this historical phenomenon. Our goal is to unravel the intricacies that underlie these conquests by examining primary sources, archaeological evidence, and scholarly interpretations of them.

This paper aims to identify some of these factors through a comparative analysis of various historical accounts that led to Islamic expansion into Europe and how they went about it by gaining control over territories. Studying military campaigns, diplomatic moves and socio-cultural interactions during this time can help us understand power dynamics, identity formation and coexistence among religious and ethnic communities. This part will also discuss the difficulties and limitations of reconstructing the history of Islamic conquests in Europe due to bias in sources and interpretive frameworks used to narrate these events. We aim to give a broad overview of the research landscape and ongoing debates about the importance of Islamic presence in Europe by examining critically how historians and archaeologists have reconstructed this period.

Islamic Conquests in Europe: A summary of the significant conquests and their impact on the European landscape

The Islamic conquests in Europe were a watershed moment in its history, shaping its geopolitical trajectory for centuries to come. From the beginning of the 7th century onwards, Islamic forces rapidly expanded their territories across the Mediterranean into central Europe. Among them was Spain, where Muslim armies quickly overran the Iberian Peninsula, establishing a powerful caliphate that lasted for many centuries.

The Islamic conquests were highly influential, not only in terms of territorial control but also in cultural and intellectual exchange. European Islamic rulers encouraged a rich cultural environment that combined aspects of Arabic, Persian, and European traditions. This blending of cultures led to a vibrant artistic and scholarly renaissance, with places such as Córdoba, Toledo and Granada becoming centres of learning and innovation.

Governance and administration also experienced significant changes during the Islamic conquests. Muslim rulers introduced decentralised rule, which allowed local leaders autonomy while maintaining central authority through appointed governors.

Within the caliphate, this system allowed for some religious and ethnic diversity, resulting in a relatively stable society with relative prosperity.

Lastly, the Islamic conquests promoted East-West ideas plus technology exchanges, leading to improvements in astronomy, mathematics as well as medicine, among other fields. European scholars translated Arabic texts into Latin, hence introducing new concepts plus discoveries that would later form the basis of the Renaissance.

In Europe, the Islamic conquests had a long-lasting impact on its culture, society and intellectual development. The influence of this era is still felt today, even after the decline of Islamic rule in Europe, which demonstrates the lasting effects of cross-cultural interactions and collaborations.

Socio-Political Shifts: Analysis of the changes in power dynamics and governance structures resulting from the Islamic conquests

The political structures of Europe were significantly altered by the Islamic conquests, leading to major socio-political shifts in power and governance. The expansion of Islam into new territories brought it into contact with different cultures and societies and led to complex political systems.

One consequence was that new administrative systems were established in conquered areas as a result of the Islamic conquest. Muslim rulers introduced hybrid models of administration that often drew upon local customs while incorporating elements of Islam. This blending resulted in multicultural societies with unique political arrangements emerging.

The Islamic conquests also led to the transformation of social hierarchies and power dynamics within the conquered regions. The infusion of Islamic rulers and administrators resulted in new elites who exercised power on the basis of religious loyalty and adherence to the Islamic caliphate. This change in power relations challenged existing social orders and caused changes in society that affected both the ruling classes and common people.

Moreover, the Islamic conquests promoted cultural interaction and knowledge transfer that impacted Europe's socio-political landscape. Interaction between Islam and Europe facilitated the exchange of ideas, technology, and administrative practices, leading to innovations in diverse areas such as architecture, science, and governance, among others. This cultural interchange not only enhanced these societies but also contributed to the political systems' evolution within conquered territories.

In conclusion, the socio-political shifts resulting from Islamic conquests in Europe were a complex mix of power dynamics, governance structures, and cultural influences. These transformations had a lasting effect beyond the conquest period itself, influencing European politics and shaping history significantly.

The cultural exchange: a study on the flow of ideas, art, and knowledge between Islamic and European societies in this era

Islamic conquests in Europe led to significant exchanges of ideas, art, and knowledge between Islamic and European societies. This cultural interchange had long-lasting effects on both regions, shaping their artistic, intellectual, and social landscapes.

One of the most important areas of cultural exchange was science and philosophy. Islamic scholars preserved classical Greek and Roman texts which had been lost to Europe during the Middle Ages. These translations helped to ignite a rebirth of learning in Europe called the Renaissance, which laid the foundation for modern scientific advances.

This period also saw an interchange of artistic influences between Islamic and European cultures. The intricate geometric patterns and bright colours used in Islamic art inspired European artists as well as craftsmen. Examples include cathedral architecture as well as palace designs or decorative objects.

Islamic conquests also facilitated cultural interactions in daily life apart from intellectual and artistic exchange. There was an exchange of food, clothing, music, and social customs between Islamic and European communities that resulted in a mixture of cultures whose traditions continue to influence each other even today.

In conclusion, the conquests led to significant cultural interaction between Islamic and European societies, which has had far-reaching implications for both regions. It promoted cross-cultural understanding, enriched artistic expression, and contributed to the advancement of knowledge and civilisation.

Economic Implications: Discussion of the economic impact of the conquests on trade routes, industries, and wealth distribution

The Islamic conquests in Europe had significant economic implications, shaping trade routes, industries, and wealth distribution during this period. The establishment of Islamic rule in various regions led to the growth of trade networks, facilitated by the expansion of Islamic territories and the development of new commercial centres. Islamic merchants played a crucial role in connecting Europe with the wider Islamic world, leading to an exchange of goods, technologies, and ideas.

The Islamic conquests also had a transformative impact on industries in conquered territories. Islamic rulers introduced advanced agricultural techniques, irrigation systems, and new crops, leading to increased productivity and economic prosperity. This agricultural innovation not only boosted local economies but also contributed to the development of trade networks that spanned across different regions.

Furthermore, the Islamic conquests led to the flourishing of urban centres and the establishment of vibrant marketplaces. Cities such as Córdoba, Toledo, and Constantinople became thriving hubs of commerce, attracting merchants, artisans, and scholars from diverse backgrounds. This urbanisation phenomenon contributed to the growth of industries such as textiles, ceramics, and metalworking, stimulating economic growth and cultural exchange.

The economic impact of the Islamic conquests extended beyond trade and industries to wealth distribution. Islamic rulers implemented policies that promoted economic prosperity and social welfare, such as the establishment of charitable foundations, support for education, and investment in public infrastructure. This focus on economic development and social welfare contributed to the overall stability and prosperity of the conquered territories, fostering a conducive environment for trade and economic growth.

In conclusion, the economic implications of the Islamic conquests in Europe were multifaceted, shaping trade routes, industries, and wealth distribution in significant ways. The integration of Islamic and European societies fostered a dynamic economic landscape marked by innovation, cultural exchange, and socioeconomic development.

Religious Interactions: Exploration of the religious shifts and interactions between Islam and Christianity in the conquered territories

Religious interactions between Islam and Christianity in the conquered territories were complex and multifaceted. The Islamic conquests in Europe brought about significant changes in the religious landscape of the region, leading to a period of transition and interaction between Islamic and Christian communities.

One key aspect of this religious interaction was the coexistence of multiple faiths in the conquered territories. While Islamic rulers established their authority over these lands, they often allowed Christian communities to practise their faith and maintain their religious institutions. This tolerance towards religious minorities helped to foster a sense of religious diversity and pluralism in the conquered territories.

At the same time, the spread of Islam in Europe also led to the conversion of some Christians to Islam. This conversion process was influenced by various factors, including social, political, and economic considerations. Some Christians may have converted to Islam to align themselves with the ruling elite or to gain social and economic advantages in the new Muslim-dominated society.

Conversely, there were also instances of Muslims converting to Christianity in the conquered territories. These conversions were sometimes motivated by personal convictions or relationships with Christian communities. The interactions between Islamic and Christian religious leaders also played a role in shaping religious attitudes and beliefs among the population.

Despite these interactions and conversions, tensions and conflicts between Islamic and Christian communities were not uncommon. Religious differences often fuelled social and political unrest, leading to periods of conflict and competition between the two faiths. However, there were also instances of cooperation and dialogue between Islamic and Christian scholars, leading to the exchange of ideas and knowledge between the two religious traditions.

Overall, the religious interactions between Islam and Christianity in the conquered territories were dynamic and complex, shaping the religious landscape of Europe for centuries to come. These interactions left a lasting impact on the cultural and religious heritage of the region, highlighting the importance of understanding the historical context of religious diversity and exchange in shaping the identities of European societies.

Military Strategies: Overview of the key military tactics employed by Islamic forces during the conquests

The Islamic forces employed a variety of strategic military tactics during the conquests in Europe. One key strategy was the effective use of cavalry, which played a crucial role in the swift movement and surprise attacks that characterised many of the conquests. Islamic armies, known for their skilled horsemen and rapid manoeuvres, were able to outmanoeuvre their opponents and achieve strategic advantages on the battlefield.

In addition to cavalry tactics, Islamic forces also utilised innovative siege techniques to overcome fortified European cities. Engineers and architects developed advanced siege weapons, such as trebuchets and battering rams, to breach city walls and force surrender. These siege tactics often struck fear into the hearts of defenders and helped ensure the success of the conquests.

Furthermore, the Islamic forces were adept at leveraging their knowledge of geography and terrain to their advantage. By utilising natural barriers and chokepoints, such as mountain passes and river crossings, they were able to control key strategic points and cut off enemy supply lines. This mastery of terrain played a significant role in the success of many conquest campaigns.

Moreover, the Islamic forces demonstrated a high level of adaptability and resourcefulness in their military strategies. They were quick to incorporate new technologies and tactics into their arsenal, constantly evolving their approach to warfare in response to changing circumstances. This flexibility and willingness to innovate gave them a distinct advantage on the battlefield.

Overall, the military strategies employed by Islamic forces during the conquests in Europe were marked by a combination of speed, precision, innovation, and adaptability. These tactics played a crucial role in the success of the conquests and left a lasting impact on the history of Europe.

Economic Implications: Discussion of the economic impact of the conquests on trade routes, industries, and wealth distribution

The Islamic conquests in Europe had significant economic implications, shaping trade routes, industries, and wealth distribution during this period. The establishment of Islamic rule in different parts led to the development of trading networks, which were facilitated by the territorial expansion of Islam and the growth of new commercial centres. The Islamic merchants played a critical role in linking Europe with the whole Islamic world, leading to the exchange of goods, technologies, and ideas.

On top of that, there was a transformation in industries within conquered territories as a result of Islamic conquests. Advanced agricultural techniques, including irrigation systems and new crops, were introduced by Islamic rulers, thereby leading to increased productivity and economic prosperity. This agricultural innovation not only boosted local economies but also contributed to the development of trade networks that spanned across different regions.

Furthermore, urban centres thrived due to Islamic conquerors' activities, which led to the establishment of vibrant marketplaces. Cities such as Córdoba, Toledo, and Constantinople became thriving hubs for commerce, attracting merchants from diverse backgrounds, artisans, and scholars alike. This phenomenon contributed to industrial growth in textiles, ceramics, and metalworking, thus stimulating economic growth as well as cultural diffusion.

The economic effect of Islamic conquests went beyond trade and industry to wealth distribution. Policies by Islamic rulers that were aimed at promoting economic prosperity and social welfare included establishing endowments, promoting education, and developing public infrastructure. The focus on economic development and social welfare contributed to the overall stability and prosperity of the conquered territories, which created an enabling environment for trade and economic growth.

In conclusion, the economic implications of the Islamic conquests in Europe were multifaceted as they shaped trade routes, industries, and wealth distribution in significant ways. The integration of Islamic and European societies led to a vibrant economy characterised by innovation, cultural interactions, and socio-economic development.

Religious Interactions: Exploration of the religious shifts and interactions between Islam and Christianity in the conquered territories

The religious interactions between Islam and Christianity in the conquered territories were intricate in many aspects. The Islamic conquests in Europe resulted in major changes within the religious landscape of this region, whereby there was a transition period as well as interaction between Muslim communities and their Christian counterparts.

The coexistence of multiple religions in the conquered territories was one main aspect of this religious interaction. However, the Islamic rulers who took over these lands usually allowed Christians to keep their churches and practice their faith. This helped in creating a sense of religious diversity and pluralism among people living in the conquered territories.

The conversion of some Christians to Islam also occurred when Islam spread to Europe. The process of conversion to Islam was influenced by various factors, including social, political, and economic considerations. Some Christians may have converted to Islam in order to be part of the ruling class or gain social and economic benefits in the new Muslim-dominated society.

On the other hand, there were situations where Muslims embraced Christianity after they had been conquered. These conversions sometimes happened due to personal conviction or association with Christian communities. The interactions between Islamic and Christian religious leaders also played a role in shaping religious attitudes and beliefs among the population.

Tensions and conflicts between Islamic and Christian communities were not uncommon despite these interactions and conversions. In this regard, social and political unrest was often ignited by religious differences, leading to periods of conflict and competition between the two religions. However, there were also cases of cooperation and dialogue among Islamic and Christian scholars that led to the exchange of ideas and knowledge between the two religious traditions.

In summary, the religious interactions that occurred in the conquered territories between Islam and Christianity were very dynamic and complex, shaping Europe's religious landscape for centuries to come. These interactions had a lasting effect on the cultural and religious heritage of the region, thus underlining the significance of appreciating historical context in relation to religious diversity as well as exchange in shaping European societies' identities.

Military Strategies: A review of the main military tactics employed by Islamic forces during the conquests

Islamic forces applied various strategic military tactics during their conquests in Europe. One important method was the efficient employment of cavalry, which was instrumental in the rapid movement and surprise attacks that characterised many of these conquests. The Islamic armies, known for their skilled horsemen and quick manoeuvres, were able to outflank their enemies and gain tactical advantages on the battlefields.

Other than cavalry tactics, Islamic forces also used innovative siege methods to capture fortified European cities. Engineers and architects designed improved siege weapons like trebuchets and battering rams that could breach city walls and force surrender. These siege techniques often struck terror into defenders' hearts, thus ensuring successful conquests.

Moreover, the Islamic forces were masters at exploiting geography and terrain to their advantage. They controlled key strategic points by using natural barriers and chokepoints such as mountain passes or river crossings. This knowledge of terrain played a major role in many successful campaigns of conquest.

The Islamic forces showed a high level of adaptability and resourcefulness in their military strategies. They quickly adopted new technologies and tactics, ever-changing their approach to warfare in response to different circumstances. This flexibility and readiness to innovate gave them an edge on the battlefield.

On the whole, the military strategies used by Islamic forces during the conquests in Europe were characterised by a combination of speed, precision, innovation and adaptability. These tactics were instrumental to the success of the conquests and have had a lasting impact on European history.

Legacy and Memory: Assessing the Lasting Impact of Islamic Conquests on European History & Collective Memory

The Islamic conquests left a deep imprint on European history and collective memory. The legacies of these conquests are intricate as they have influenced European societies' development in various ways. One important aspect of this legacy is a cultural exchange between Islamic civilisation and Europe. The Islamic conquests facilitated knowledge, art, and ideas transmission between these two worlds, leading to a rich cross-fertilisation among cultures.

Moreover, Europe was greatly affected economically by the Islamic conquests as they changed trade routes and commerce for centuries to come. The newly created trade networks and economic systems brought about by Islamic forces set the stage for new industries to emerge and wealth to grow in European territories.

Religiously, Islam was involved with Christianity during the Islamic conquests. This diversity of religions and coexistence has a long-term effect on religious identities and practices in Europe that have contributed to the rich tapestry of religious beliefs and traditions existing in Europe today.

The military tactics used by Muslims during these invasions have had a lasting impact on European warfare. The innovative strategies employed by Muslim armies influenced European military thought and tactics, which shaped warfare development in this region.

In general, the legacy of Islamic conquests in Europe is intricate and multifaceted, with far-reaching consequences for European history and collective memory. By examining the aftermath of these invasions, we can get a better understanding of the diverse tapestry of European history and culture.

The Islamic conquests in Europe were transformative and dynamic, influencing the continent in deeply varied ways depending on the region. The diversity of outcomes, shaped by local contexts and geo-political realities, underscores the complexity of this historical period and its lasting legacy.

Regional Variations: A Closer Analysis

In the Iberian Peninsula, the conquest by the Umayyad Caliphate culminated in the establishment of Al-Andalus, a flourishing centre of scientific, philosophical, and artistic innovation. Advancements in fields like astronomy, medicine, literature, and architecture flourished under Islamic rule, with cities such as Córdoba becoming hubs of intellectual synthesis that attracted scholars from across Europe and the Islamic world. The coexistence of diverse religious communities under the framework of dhimma agreements, while not without tension, fostered a unique multicultural dynamic across the region. This legacy of cultural cross-pollination left an indelible imprint on the Iberian identity, even after the Reconquista.

In Southern France, the Islamic conquests faced staunch resistance from Frankish forces under leaders such as Charles Martel, most famously at the Battle of Tours (732 CE). Unlike Iberia, where integration and settlement took root, the incursions into Southern France were characterised by swift raids and fleeting control. The fragmented power structures of the region, combined with decisive counterattacks, meant that Islamic influence was more transient, leaving fewer lasting cultural impacts than in Al-Andalus. The encounters here, however, played a significant role in shaping European perceptions of Islam as a formidable martial and ideological force.

Turning to the Balkans and Greece, the Byzantine Empire emerged as one of the most stubborn adversaries of Islamic expansion. The Umayyad and later Abbasid forces targeted Constantinople, the heart of Byzantine power, due to its immense strategic importance as a bridge between Europe and Asia. The prolonged sieges of the city, particularly in 717–718 CE, demonstrated not only Islamic military might but also Byzantine resilience, diplomacy, and defensive ingenuity. The Byzantines' use of Greek fire and entrenched fortifications allowed the empire to withstand Islamic advances, preserving a bastion of Christian power amid mounting pressure from both east and west.

In Sicily and Southern Italy, the Islamic conquests resulted in a remarkable exchange of cultures through overlapping Arab, Norman, Byzantine, and later Latin influences. As an island at the crossroads of the Mediterranean, Sicily became a melting pot of knowledge and aesthetics. Under Islamic rule, agricultural innovations such as improved irrigation and crop introduction (e.g., citrus fruits) transformed local economies. Furthermore, the fusion of architectural traditions—exemplified by Palermo's Norman-Arab-Byzantine structures—captured the hybrid legacy of this era, which resonated long after Islamic dominance waned.

Concluding Remarks: Reflections on the Broader Impact

The diversity of experiences across Iberia, Southern France, the Balkans, and Sicily illustrates the multi-layered nature of the Islamic conquests. These regional variations not only showcase the adaptability and ingenuity of Islamic forces but also reveal the complexity of Europe's response to this wave of expansion.

From a cultural perspective, the exchange of ideas, artistry, and technologies between Islamic and European societies stands out as one of the era's defining legacies. Al-Andalus serves as a paradigm of how intellectual exchange can thrive amidst religious and cultural diversity, seeding developments that would later help to catalyse Europe's Renaissance. Similarly, the architectural and agricultural imprints in Sicily emphasise how cross-cultural interactions transcended mere military conquests, fostering enduring innovations.

Economically, the Islamic incursions disrupted and then redefined trade networks, linking Europe more directly to the broader Islamic world. Trade routes connecting the Mediterranean with North Africa, the Middle East, and even Asia flourished, facilitating the exchange of goods, technologies, and knowledge. This economic integration was not just a transactional phenomenon but a transformative process that contributed to long-term European growth.

Militarily, the Islamic conquests revealed both the strengths and limitations of early medieval warfare. The incorporation of advanced tactics and technologies by Islamic forces often outmatched fragmented European defences. However, resistance—most notably in Southern France and the Byzantine Empire—proved that geography, local alliances, and strategic foresight could provide effective countermeasures against even well-coordinated invasions.

Religiously and ideologically, the conquests highlighted the dynamic interactions between Islam and Christianity during this formative period. In some cases, coexistence led to syncretism and gradual cultural blending, as seen in Al-Andalus, while in others, such as the Balkans, it hardened boundaries, reinforcing a sense of religious and cultural competition. The interplay between resistance and accommodation ultimately shaped the evolving religious identities of both conquerors and the conquered.

In synthesis, the Islamic conquests in Europe did not unfold as a monolithic campaign of domination but rather as a series of intricate and regionally specific encounters. These conquests profoundly shaped the trajectory of European history, fostering mutual transformations that resonated well beyond the medieval period. The enduring legacy of this era lies not only in the battles fought or territories held but also in the vibrant exchanges of ideas, culture, and innovation that bridged civilisational divides. Such interactions remind us that history, even when marked by conflict, holds the potential for enrichment and enduring influence.

Chapter 15

Reflections on significance

The Context

The Islamic conquests of medieval Europe totally reshaped the region and had a long-lasting effect. The military campaigns expanded Islamic territories and significantly influenced Europe's culture, society, and politics. Therefore, understanding the historical importance of these events requires examining their background.

Islam emerged as a powerful new force in the Mediterranean world during the 7th century. Religious zeal and territorial aggrandisement inspired early Islamic conquerors to undertake military expeditions that quickly spread across North Africa and the Middle East. In Europe, by the 8th Century, Muslims had begun embarking on a series of conquests which would eventually leave an indelible mark on this continent.

The Islamic conquests in Europe were not isolated events but part of a broader historical narrative that included political, religious, and cultural dynamics. For instance, the conquest of Spain marked the beginning of centuries of Islamic rule on the

Iberian Peninsula, during which Muslim rulers presided over a diverse and prosperous society that amalgamated Arab, Berber, and European cultures.

As Islam spread into Southern France and the Balkans, it encountered different populations with their own customs and identities. The resulting clash between civilisations resulted in a complicated mix of cooperation, conflict and cultural exchange. For example, the two sieges on Constantinople in 717-718 and again in 1453 revealed how important this city was as a meeting point between East and West, hence its continuing influence under Islamic rule.

Islamic conquests in Europe had far-reaching consequences beyond military victories, including economic, social, and intellectual transformations. Trade networks thrived, connecting distant regions and allowing goods, ideas and technologies to be traded. Artistic styles from the Islamic world have transformed European culture through architectural practices as well as urban landscapes.

Historical Impact of Islamic Conquests in Europe

The Islamic conquests in Europe during the medieval period had a profound impact on the region's history and development. These military campaigns, led by the expanding Islamic caliphates, brought about significant changes in the political, social, cultural, and economic landscape of Europe. The conquests resulted in the establishment of Islamic rule in various parts of the continent, shaping its future in numerous ways.

Among the major historical effects of Islamic conquests in Europe was the establishment of new political entities and power structures. They resulted in the creation of Islamic emirates and caliphates in various regions like Spain, Sicily, and parts of the Balkans. These Muslim-controlled territories were instrumental in shaping Europe's geopolitics, determining relations between different kingdoms and empires.

European culture and society have been influenced by the Islamic conquests to this day. The interactions between Muslims and non-Muslims resulted in an exchange of ideas, technologies, and artistic traditions. Scholars from Islam made significant contributions to science, philosophy, and medicine, among others, thus introducing new knowledge and innovations into European society.

Moreover, there was a significant economic impact that resulted from the Islamic conquests in Europe. The Muslim-ruled territories became important centres for trade, linking Europe with other parts of the Islamic world. This led to increased exchange of goods, technologies and ideas, hence enhancing economic prosperity for many areas under Islamic rule.

The conquests also had religious implications, as the spread of Islam in Europe resulted in the coexistence of different religious communities. This diversity of faiths contributed to a rich cultural tapestry and fostered a spirit of religious tolerance in some areas. However, it also led to tensions and conflicts between Muslims, Christians, and Jews in certain regions.

In conclusion, the historical impact of the Islamic conquests in Europe was multifaceted and far-reaching. The conquests not only reshaped the political and cultural landscape of the continent but also laid the foundation for future developments in various fields. The legacy of Islamic rule in Europe continues to be felt to this day, reflecting the complex and dynamic interactions between different civilisations during the medieval period.

Influence on European Culture and Society

The Islamic conquests in Europe had a profound influence on European culture and society. The encounter with Islamic civilisation brought new perspectives and knowledge that deeply impacted various aspects of European life. One significant area of influence was in the fields of science, mathematics, and philosophy. Islamic scholars preserved and transmitted ancient texts, contributing to the European Renaissance and the scientific revolution.

Islamic architecture and design also left a lasting mark on Europe. The intricate geometric patterns, innovative use of light and space, and decorative motifs influenced European architecture, particularly evident in the Moorish architecture of Spain.

Moreover, the Islamic conquests fostered cultural exchange and trade networks, leading to the introduction of new foods, spices, and textiles in Europe. This intercultural exchange enriched European cuisine, fashion, and daily life.

The Islamic conquests also influenced European language and literature. Arabic words and literary forms were integrated into European languages, and the tales of Arabic literature such as "One Thousand and One Nights" held captive the imagination of Europeans who later produced other literary works inspired by them.

Furthermore, the Islamic conquests challenged existing social structures and hierarchies in Europe. The encounter with Islamic societies with more advanced governance systems and legal structures prompted European rulers to reform their own systems, leading to the development of centralised monarchies as well as legal codes.

In conclusion, the influence of the Islamic conquests on European culture and society was multifaceted and profound. The encounter with Islamic civilisation enriched European knowledge in terms of architecture, cuisine, literature, and social structures, which shaped European history, thus laying the foundation for a more interconnected, diverse Europe.

Political Consequences of Islamic Rule

The political consequences of the Islamic conquests in Europe were far-reaching and changed the power relations across the continent. The arrival of Islamic rule in different areas resulted in a complex interplay of alliances, conflicts and shifts in governance that had long-lasting effects on Europe's political landscape.

Another major outcome was the emergence of new power structures. Islamic rulers achieved their dominance through a combination of military power, diplomacy, and administrative systems. This led to the establishment of various political units which often co-existed with existing European kingdoms and empires.

Islamic rule also fostered cultural and intellectual exchanges that influenced political decision-making. European rulers and officials were influenced by new ideas, technologies, and administrative practices brought by Islamic scholars and administrators. Such cross-cultural encounters enhanced the quality of political discourse and contributed to shaping new policies and strategies.

On top of that, political stability was significantly affected by the economic prosperity brought about by Islamic trade networks and economic innovations. The wealth generated through trade flowed into the coffers of Islamic rulers, enabling them to consolidate their power and influence. This economic strength often translated into military might, allowing Islamic rulers to assert their authority and expand their territories.

However, the consequences of Islamic rule on politics were not homogeneous throughout Europe. In some areas, there were long wars and opposition from local people after Islamic conquests; this led to political instability and uprisings. Conversely, in other places, it served as a source of stability and prosperity, leading to alliances between European powers and Muslim rulers.

In conclusion, the political implications of Islamic rule in Europe were complex and varied, hence affecting socio-political dynamics for centuries ahead. The interaction between power, culture, and economy under Islam laid the foundation for a new era of political development and interaction, which still affects European politics today.

Economic Transformations and Trade Networks

The Islamic conquests in Europe led to significant economic transformations and the creation of vast trade networks that defied cultural and religious borders. Cordoba, Seville, Granada (Spain), as well as Cairo, Constantinople, and Palermo, were thriving commercial centres under Islamic rule. These cities became important links between East and West, facilitating the movement of goods, ideas, and technology.

To boost their economies, Islamic rulers put in place policies like building complex infrastructures such as irrigation systems, roads and markets. They also promoted a good atmosphere for business by ensuring safe trade routes, standardising weights and measures, and encouraging different industries.

The Islamic conquests led to the integration of various regions into a vast network of trade routes called the Silk Road, which was one of the major aspects of economic transformations. This network connected Europe, Asia and Africa, thus allowing for the exchange of luxury goods such as silk, spices and precious metals. The Islamic rulers facilitated this trade by creating safe passage for merchants and a stable economic environment.

Moreover, the Islamic conquests also brought about new financial instruments and banking practices that completely changed business transactions. For instance, innovations like letters of credit, bills of exchange, and partnerships have made it easier and more secure for merchants to engage in long-distance trades. These practices not only enabled economic transactions but also encouraged cultural interactions between different communities.

In conclusion, the European continent's economic development was influenced by the economic transformations and trade networks established during the Islamic conquests, as well as the commercial practices shaped by them; these factors also contributed to knowledge transfer across borders.

Religious Tensions and Coexistence

During the Islamic conquests in Europe, religious tensions were a common phenomenon where different faiths clashed and coexisted within the same territories. The coming of Islamic rulers often raised fears among Christian and Jewish communities, who thought that they would be persecuted or forced to convert. However, historical records also showcase religious tolerance and peaceful coexistence among these diverse religious groups.

One of the most notable examples of religious tensions was in Spain, where Christians, Muslims, and Jews lived together. The Reconquista, which was a series of Christian campaigns to regain control over the Iberian Peninsula, resulted in increased hostility between different religious communities. This period witnessed conflicts for dominance in religion as well as control over sacred places, thereby causing deep-rooted hatred.

Apart from these tensions, there were also moments when religious cooperation and coexistence prevailed. For instance, some Islamic rulers in Spain, like the Umayyad Caliphate of Córdoba, had policies that allowed Christians and Jews to practice their religions, although with some restrictions. It thus led to cultural exchange and intellectual blossoming since scholars from various religious backgrounds interacted with each other, sharing knowledge.

In the Balkans and Greece, similar religious dynamics were brought about by the conquests of Islamic forces. Orthodox Christian populations faced challenges under Islamic rule, but there were also instances of religious tolerance and coexistence. The Ottoman Empire, in particular, implemented a system known as the millet system, which gave autonomy to different communities, thus fostering religious pluralism.

The cultural and architectural heritage of Europe still bears witness to these religious tensions and coexistence. This period saw complex interactions between various faith traditions, evidenced by the fusion of Islamic, Christian, and Jewish influences in art, architecture, and literature. It is a legacy that reminds us of Europe's history as a rich tapestry of religious diversity and coexistence.

Military Strategies and Legacy

The military strategies that were employed during the Islamic conquests in Europe had far-reaching consequences for world history. Arab armies used speed, manoeuvrability, and adaptability to outwit their enemies. One notable tactic was employing light cavalry units called "Ribaat", which proved very effective in quick strikes or hit-and-run tactics.

Another military innovation was the use of siege warfare, where advanced siege engines and techniques were used by

Arabs to capture fortified cities and strongholds. Through tunnels, battering rams, and siege towers, they were able to breach enemy defences and secure victory.

Additionally, the Arabs incorporated diplomacy and strategic alliances in their military campaigns by often taking advantage of local discontent or rivalries that weakened their adversaries from within. This combination of military force with diplomatic manoeuvring enabled the Arab armies to expand their territories quickly and establish long-lasting rule over conquered lands.

The legacy of these military strategies is evident in how much they influenced the region. The Arab conquests changed Europe's geopolitical landscape by establishing new dynasties and shifting power balances. Also, future generations of military leaders and strategists would draw upon the military innovations introduced by Arab armies, which left an indelible mark on the art of war.

In general, this section demonstrates how effective innovative thinking, adaptability, and strategic planning are when applied in warfare during Islamic invasions in Europe. This chapter underscores why it is important for us to study past military campaigns so as to understand them within a broader historical context while shaping modern-day military strategies.

Intellectual and Scientific Contributions

Significant intellectual and scientific contributions were made during the Islamic conquests in Europe, which had a lasting impact on this area. Muslim scholars made great strides in various fields, including mathematics, astronomy, medicine, and philosophy. One of the most important figures of that time was Al-Kindi, a Persian polymath who is often called "the father of Arab philosophy." In metaphysics, psychology, and ethics, Al-

Kindi made significant contributions that laid the foundation for future developments in Islamic philosophy.

Another influential figure was the Persian mathematician Al-Khwarizmi, whose work on algebra provided the basis for modern algebraic methods. The concept of algebraic equations and algorithms was introduced by his treatise on algebra entitled Hisab al-Jabr w'al-Muqabala, which revolutionised mathematics in Europe.

Islamic astronomers also made substantial advancements during this period, developing sophisticated instruments for measuring time and predicting celestial movements. Scholars such as Al-Battani and Al-Zarqali refined astronomical knowledge and navigation techniques.

The practice of medicine in Islam made great strides through the contributions of Islamic physicians like Ibn Sina (Avicenna) and Ibn al-Nafis. The Canon of Medicine by Ibn Sina became a cornerstone in the development of medical science as it combined ancient Greek and Persian medical knowledge with Islamic elements.

The Islamic conquests in Europe not only reshaped the political and territorial boundaries of the medieval period but also ushered in one of the most transformative cultural exchanges in the continent's history. Their intellectual, artistic, and architectural legacies remain deeply significant, having had a profound impact on the development of European identity and the trajectory of its intellectual, artistic, and economic progress. Below, I explore these enduring influences more comprehensively:

Intellectual and Scientific Contributions

The Islamic conquests brought extensive intellectual and scientific advancements that redefined Europe's scholarly traditions. Islamic scholars played a pivotal role in preserving, expanding upon, and transmitting ancient knowledge. By translating foundational Greek texts (such as those by Aristotle, Plato, and Galen) into Arabic and, subsequently, Latin, they ensured the survival and dissemination of ideas that would have otherwise been lost to Europe during its early medieval period.

The Islamic Golden Age was characterised by significant developments in fields like mathematics (for example, the popularisation of Arabic numerals and algebra), astronomy (with improved astrolabe designs and extensive star charts), and medicine (as outlined in Avicenna's *Canon of Medicine*, which became a standard text in European universities for centuries). These contributions served as a catalyst for Europe's later intellectual flowering during the Renaissance and Scientific Revolution. In this way, the legacy of Islamic scholarship forms a critical bridge between antiquity and modernity in Europe.

Artistic and Architectural Influences

Islamic conquests introduced a distinctive artistic and architectural vocabulary to Europe, with a blend of Islamic, Byzantine, and local traditions giving rise to some of the continent's most remarkable structures. The **Great Mosque of Cordoba** (the Mezquita) remains a shining example of this cultural and aesthetic exchange. Its characteristic horseshoe arches, expansive hypostyle hall, and lavish ornamentation reflect the sophisticated design principles of Islamic architecture.

Similarly, the **Alhambra in Granada** serves as a testament to the advanced craftsmanship and artistic vision of the period. Its intricate geometric patterns, complex arabesques, and poetic inscriptions capture a unique blend of utility, spirituality, and beauty, inspiring European architects and artists for centuries.

Islamic art also introduced decorative techniques such as calligraphy, arabesques, and elaborate tilework, which influenced European forms of design. These elements began appearing not only in art but also in textiles and sculpture, subtly permeating the artistic traditions of medieval and Renaissance Europe. Artists and craftsmen adapted these elements, enriching the European artistic landscape and promoting a cross-cultural synthesis of aesthetic ideals.

Cultural Interactions and Multiculturalism

One of the defining legacies of the Islamic conquests was the creation of multicultural societies in regions like Al-Andalus. Here, Muslims, Christians, and Jews coexisted, interacted, and contributed to vibrant centres of learning, trade, and culture. While this coexistence was not without tension, it fostered periods of intellectual synergy and mutual respect that influenced European approaches to culture and governance.

This historical period offers a notable precedent for modern ideas of pluralism and multiculturalism. The spirit of coexistence that characterised Al-Andalus has inspired centuries of interfaith dialogue and collaborative scholarship, serving as a model for societies navigating religious and cultural diversity today.

Economic and Trade Networks

The economic impact of Islamic conquests on Europe cannot be overstated. By integrating Europe into vast trade networks that extended across the Islamic world and into Asia and Africa, these conquests significantly enhanced commerce in Europe. Goods such as silk, spices, perfumes, and scientific instruments flowed into Europe, profoundly impacting European economies, tastes, and technological advancements.

Moreover, the introduction of advanced agricultural techniques—such as irrigation systems and the cultivation of new crops like citrus fruits, sugarcane, and cotton—had a transformative effect on European agriculture, increasing yields and diversifying diets. These changes laid the groundwork for future economic developments that would shape Europe in profound ways.

Long-Term Significance in Modern Europe

The legacies of the Islamic conquests are still keenly felt in modern-day Europe, particularly through the physical presence of architectural wonders like the Alhambra and the Great Mosque of Cordoba, both of which continue to attract admiration and scholarly inquiry. Contemporary architects and artists draw inspiration from Islamic designs, perpetuating a tradition of cross-cultural aesthetics in both public and private spaces.

Furthermore, the intellectual exchange that began during the Islamic conquests set the stage for Europe's evolving traditions of learning and inquiry. The emphasis on logic, reason, and empirical observation introduced by Islamic thinkers remains a cornerstone of modern scientific and philosophical thought.

On a societal level, the Islamic conquests underscore Europe's historical interconnectedness with the wider world, challenging insular narratives and highlighting the contributions of Islamic culture to the continent's shared heritage. By acknowledging and celebrating this history, modern Europe can foster a more inclusive narrative that values diversity as a source of strength.

Conclusion

The Islamic conquests in Europe were not solely a matter of military campaigns or territorial expansions; they initiated a unique and enduring exchange of ideas, technologies, and cultural practices. From the preservation and expansion of ancient knowledge to the flourishing of art and architecture that blended stylistic traditions, the impact of this period is irrefutable. Today, the legacies of these conquests remain visible in Europe's intellectual traditions, artistic achievements, and cultural diversity, offering important lessons on the value of interconnectedness and mutual inspiration in shaping a richer, more inclusive future.

Bibliography

Arabic References

المصادر التاريخية القديمة

من المهم ملاحظة أن هذه المصادر غالباً ما تُنشر بتحقيقات ودراسات حديثة، لذا سأذكر اسم المحقق أو المُعلق إن وجد:

ابن عبد الحكم (أبو القاسم عبد الرحمن بن عبد الله بن عبد الحكم المصري):
فتوح مصر وأخبارها. الكتاب متوفر بتحقيقات عديدة، منها تحقيق:
تشارلز توري: صدر عن مطبعة ليدن في هولندا عام 1920م.
تحقيق: علي محمد عمر: صدر عن مكتبة الثقافة الدينية في القاهرة.

ابن القوطية (محمد بن عمر بن عبد العزيز القرطبي):
تاريخ افتتاح الأندلس. أيضاً من الكتب التي نُشرت بتحقيقات مختلفة، منها:
تحقيق: جوليان ريبيرا: صدر في مدريد عام 1868م.
تحقيق: إبراهيم الأبياري: صدر عن دار الكتاب المصري في القاهرة ودار الكتاب اللبناني في بيروت.

ابن الأثير (عز الدين أبو الحسن علي بن محمد الجزري):
الكامل في التاريخ: يُعتبر من أشهر كتب التاريخ الإسلامي، وقد طُبع عدة طبعات، منها:
دار صادر في بيروت: وهي من أشهر الطبعات المتداولة.
دار الكتاب العربي في بيروت.

المقري التلمساني (أبو العباس أحمد بن محمد المقري):
نفح الطيب من غصن الأندلس الرطيب: من أمهات الكتب عن تاريخ الأندلس، وقد طُبع عدة طبعات، منها:
تحقيق: إحسان عباس: صدر عن دار صادر في بيروت.
طبعة دار الكتب العلمية في بيروت.

الحميري (محمد بن عبد المنعم الحميري):
الروض المعطار في خبر الأقطار: طُبع بتحقيق:
تحقيق: إحسان عباس: صدر عن مكتبة لبنان في بيروت.

الطبري (محمد بن جرير الطبري):
يُعتبر كتابه "تاريخ الرسل والملوك" أو "تاريخ الطبري" من أهم المصادر التاريخية الإسلامية الشاملة. يغطي الكتاب تاريخ العالم من الخلق حتى أوائل القرن الرابع الهجري. يتناول الطبري فتح الأندلس في سياق الأحداث التاريخية لتلك الفترة.

ابن خلدون (عبد الرحمن بن محمد بن خلدون):
يُعتبر كتابه "العبر وديوان المبتدأ والخبر في أيام العرب والعجم والبربر ومن عاصرهم من ذوي السلطان الأكبر"، المشهور باسم "مقدمة ابن خلدون"، من أهم المؤلفات التاريخية والاجتماعية والفلسفية. يتناول ابن خلدون تاريخ الأندلس في سياق حديثه عن تاريخ البربر والدول الإسلامية في المغرب والأندلس.

الدراسات الحديثة

حسين مؤنس:
تاريخ الأندلس: صدر عن مكتبة مدبولي في القاهرة.
محمد عبد الله عنان:
دولة الإسلام في الأندلس: صدر عن مكتبة الخانجي في القاهرة.
عبد الرحمن علي الحجي:
فتح الأندلس: صدر عن دار المدار الإسلامي في بيروت.
سلوى علي:
المسلمون في الأندلس: صدر عن عالم الكتب في القاهرة.
عمر فروخ:
العرب والإسلام في الحوض الغربي من البحر الأبيض المتوسط من فتح المغرب وفتح الأندلس إلى نهاية عصر الولاة.
٥٥. الناشر: المكتب التجاري. بيروت، لبنان.
بهاء الدين محمد أسعد. جمال يوسف الخلفات: العسكرية الإسلامية وقادتها العظام.
الناشر: مكتبة المنار. الزرقاء، الأردن.

Abu-Lughod, J. L. (1989). *Before European Hegemony: The World System A.D. 1250-1350*. Oxford University Press.

Abun-Nasr, J. (2011). *A History of the Maghrib in the Islamic Period*. Cambridge University Press.

Ayalon, D. (1989). *Islamic History*. Routledge.

Babinger, F. (1992). *Mehmed the Conqueror and His Times*. Princeton University Press.

Baker, C. (2004). *The Islamic World: Past and Present*. Oxford University Press.

Balkan, F. (2023). The political dimensions of the Siege of Constantinople. *Journal of Ottoman Studies*.

Bennison, A. K. (2009). *The Great Caliphs: The Golden Age of the 'Abbasid Empire*. Yale University Press.

Berkey, J. (2003). *The Formation of Islam: Religion and Society in the Near East, 600–1800*. Cambridge University Press.

Blair, S. (2000). *Islamic Architecture: Form, Function, and Meaning*. Yale University Press.

Brett, M., & Fentress, E. (1996). *The Berbers*. Blackwell.

Brown, P. (1989). *The Rise of Western Christendom: Triumph and Diversity, AD 200-1000*. Wiley-Blackwell.

Burns, A. (2009). *Trade and Cultural Exchange in the Mediterranean during the Islamic Conquests*. Routledge.

Cabeza, J. (1995). *Al-Andalus: The History of Muslim Spain*. University of California Press.

Cerulli, M. (2011). Islamic trade networks and market mechanisms in the Middle Ages. *Journal of Economic History*.

Collins, R. (1989). *The Arab Conquest of Spain: 710–797*. Basil Blackwell.

Collins, R. (2014). *Caliphs and Kings: Spain, 796–1031*.

Courcy, M. (2019). *Medieval Merchants and Markets: Economic Life in the Middle Ages*. Palgrave Macmillan.

Crone, P. (2003). *God's Rule: Government and Islam*. Columbia University Press.

Crone, P. (2005). *God's Rule: Government and Islam*. Columbia University Press.

Davis, N. Z. (2001). *Islands of History*. University of California Press.

Dodds, J. (1992). *Al-Andalus: The Art of Islamic Spain*. The Metropolitan Museum of Art.

Eisenstadt, S. N. (1986). *The Political Systems of Empires*. Transaction Publishers.

Elias, N. (2001). *The Civilizing Process: Sociogenetic and Psychogenetic Investigations*. Wiley-Blackwell.

Esposito, J. L. (1998). *Islam: The Straight Path*. Oxford University Press.

Esposito, J. L. (1999). *The Oxford History of Islam*. Oxford University Press.

Esposito, J. L. (2016). *Islam and Politics*. Syracuse University Press.

Fierro, M. (2005). Abd al-Rahman III: The first Cordoban caliph.

Fletcher, R. (2006). *Moorish Spain*. The University of California Press.

Gaehtgens, M. (2018). The cisterns of Constantinople: Life under siege. *Byzantine Studies Quarterly*.

Gerlach, D. (2015). *Networks of Trade in the Medieval Mediterranean*. Cambridge University Press.

Gibb, H. A. R. (1963). *Islamic Society and Culture*. Oxford University Press.

Gibb, H. A. R. (1969). *Islam: A Historical and Political Analysis*. Oxford University Press.

Gill, R. (2012). *Medieval Trade and the Role of the Merchant*. *Economic History Review*.

Glick, T. F. (1999). *Islamic Science in the Middle Ages*. Hill and Wang.

Goldziher, I. (1971). *Introduction to Islamic Theology and Law*. Princeton University Press.

Griffiths, M. (2021). *Trade and Society in the Early Islamic Empire*. Cambridge University Press.

Haldon, J. (2010). *The Byzantine Wars: Battles and Campaigns of the Byzantine Era*. The History Press.

Hansen, V. (2012). *The Silk Road: A New History*. Oxford University Press.

Harrison, D. (2007). *The Historical Landscape of Southern France*. Cambridge University Press.

Hawting, G. R. (2000). *The First Dynasty of Islam: The Umayyad Caliphate AD 661–750*. Routledge.

Hodgson, M. G. S. (1974). *The Venture of Islam: Conscience and History in a World Civilization* (Vol. 1). University of Chicago Press.

Holt, P. M. (1995). *The Oxford History of Islam*. Oxford University Press.

Hourani, A. (1991). *A History of the Arab Peoples*. Harvard University Press.

Hourani, A. (2010). *A History of the Arab Peoples*.

Hoyland, R. (2014). *In God's Path: The Arab Conquests and the Creation of an Islamic Empire*. Oxford University Press.

Howard, D. (2001). *Islam and the West: A Conversation*. Routledge.

Ibn Khaldun. (1967). *The Muqaddimah: An Introduction to History*. Princeton University Press.

Ibn Khaldun, A. (1990). *The Muqaddimah: An Introduction to History*. Princeton University Press.

Ibn Khaldun. (1998). *The Muqaddimah: An Introduction to History*. Princeton University Press.

Kennedy, H. (1996). *Muslim Spain and Portugal*. Routledge.

Kennedy, H. (2004). *The Armies of the Caliphs: Military and Society in the Early Islamic State*. Routledge.

Kennedy, H. (2007). *The Great Arab Conquests: How the Spread of Islam Changed the World We Live In*. Da Capo Press.

Lapidus, I. M. (1988). *A History of Islamic Societies*. Cambridge University Press.

Lindsay, H. (2009). *The Islamic World: A History*. Wiley-Blackwell.

Mango, C. (2005). *Constantinople: City of the World's Desire*. John Wiley & Sons.

McCormick, M. (2001). *Charlemagne's Early Empire*. Cambridge University Press.

Menocal, M. R. (2002). *The Ornament of the World: How Muslims, Jews, and Christians Created a Culture of Tolerance in Medieval Spain*. Little, Brown and Company.

Pomeranz, K. (2000). *The Great Divergence: China, Europe, and the Making of the Modern World Economy*. Princeton University Press.

Riley-Smith, J. (2000). *The Crusades: A History*. The Continuum International Publishing Group Inc.

Robinson, C. (2011). *The New Cambridge History of Islam, Volume 1: The Formation of the Islamic World*. Cambridge University Press.

Shaban, M. A. (1970). *Islamic History: A New Interpretation*. Harvard University Press.

Seddon, D. (2012). *Islamic Expansion and the Cultural Exchange*. Routledge.

Tolan, J. (2013). *Saracens: Islam in the Medieval European Imagination*. Columbia University Press.

Online References:

- Sikandar shah (2023). "Robert Greene: A Process for Finding & Achieving Your Unique Purpose". https://doi.org/10.55277/researchhub.49fagxwk
- Scott Pribble (2023). "The Barter Economy of the Khmer Rouge Labor Camps". https://doi.org/10.4324/9781003346371
- Cunha, Agostinho (2024). "Warfare in the 21st century postmodern world : causes and consequences for states' survival". Instituto da Defesa Nacional. https://core.ac.uk/download/614515595.pdf
- Brittain-Hale, Amber, Brittain-Hale, Amber (2023). "Clausewitzian Theory Of War in The Age of Cognitive Warfare". Pepperdine Digital Commons. https://core.ac.uk/download/614454981.pdf
- Antczak, Anna, Sliwa, Zdzislaw (2024). "MILITARY DOMAIN AS A COMPONENT OF INFORMATION WARFARE". Sõjateadlane. https://core.ac.uk/download/611887151.pdf
- Aima Tahir, Khushboo Ejaz (2023). "Pakistan and Fourth Generation Warfare". Journal of Politics and International Studies. https://core.ac.uk/download/560702643.pdf
- Osflaten, Amund (2023). "The Russian Way of Regular Land Warfare: A Comparative Case Study of Four Major Russian Operations after the Cold War". King's College London. https://core.ac.uk/download/616581847.pdf
- Hoskins, Alexander (2024). "Red-Handed: Assessing the Deptha of Chinese Economic Espionage". SMU Scholar. https://core.ac.uk/download/624147629.pdf
- Achu, Ayuk A., Duke, Otu, Enyia, Jacob Otu, Njong, et al. (2022). "Intelligence Gathering Imperative: A Tool for Successful Security Outfits' Operation". 'Lifescience Global'. https://core.ac.uk/download/544387423.pdf
- DAR, Deni, Nuriada, Wayan, Rusyadi, Dadi (2022). "The Prince Diponegoro's war strategy from the perspective of the Indonesia total war strategy". Indonesia Defense University. https://core.ac.uk/download/539620075.pdf
- Ekah Robert Ekah (2022). "Asymmetric Warfare in Contemporary Africa: The Case of the Anglophone Secessionist Struggle in Cameroon". Global Journals Inc. (US). https://core.ac.uk/download/581122617.pdf
- Choudhury, Diptendu (2023). "The Salience of Air Power in Accelerating Land Operations Across Various Terrains". Centre For Land Warfare Studies (CLAWS), New Delhi, India. https://core.ac.uk/download/578764342.pdf
- Pezzati, Andrea (2024). "Trading space for time : the Confederate Army's strategy revisited". https://core.ac.uk/download/621690603.pdf

- Brittain-Hale, Amber, Brittain-Hale, Amber (2023). "Clausewitzian Theory Of War in The Age of Cognitive Warfare". Pepperdine Digital Commons. https://core.ac.uk/download/614454981.pdf
- Phillips, Elisabeth Jana (2023). "From Mascot to Marine: The Long Walk to the American Military Dog Program". Scholars Crossing. https://core.ac.uk/download/568249938.pdf
- Mabelitini, Charles Brian (2024). "British Fortification Strategy in the South Carolina Backcountry During the Southern Campaign of the American Revolution: Archaeological and Historical Perspectives on Infrastructure and Landscape". Scholar Commons. https://scholarcommons.sc.edu/context/etd/article/8620/viewcontent/1045519.pdf
- Bruso, Jordan J (2022). "The Siege of Calais During The Hundred Years War: An English Perspective, 1344-1347". DigitalCommons@UMaine. https://core.ac.uk/download/519803588.pdf
- Cropsey, Seth (2023). "Naval Considerations in the Russo-Ukrainian War". U.S. Naval War College Digital Commons. https://core.ac.uk/download/555441925.pdf
- (2022). "Empires of the Sea". 'Brill'. https://core.ac.uk/download/520264079.pdf
- Anderson, Ralph Thomas (2023). ""Work with the god" : military divination and rational battle-planning in Xenophon". 'Informa UK Limited'. https://core.ac.uk/download/552802238.pdf
- Comstock, Kasey James (2023). "With Sand in Their Pockets: Lessons of the American Expeditionary Force's Mobilization for the First World War". Scholars Crossing. https://core.ac.uk/download/578700649.pdf
- Crenshaw, Martha, National Counterterrorism Innovation, Technology, and Education Center, Robinson, Kaitlyn (2023). "Transnational Ties Between Selected U.S. and Foreign Violent Extremist Actors: Evidence from the Mapping Militants Project". DigitalCommons@UNO. https://core.ac.uk/download/579996708.pdf
- Malone, Iris, National Counterterrorism Innovation, Technology, and Education Center, Strouboulis, Anastasia (2022). "Emerging Risks in the Marine Transportation System (MTS), 2001- 2021". DigitalCommons@UNO. https://core.ac.uk/download/571266505.pdf
- Haines, Spencer (2022). "Defying the Nomadic versus Sedentary Dichotomy: The Rise and Fall of Zunghar Self-Strengthening Campaigns in Central Eurasia (17th-18th Centuries)". https://core.ac.uk/download/519771780.pdf

- Matar, Charles Matar (2023). "Perceptions of Naval Power in Crisis Management: Lebanon and the Levant During the Cold War". https://core.ac.uk/download/603255753.pdf

www.ingramcontent.com/pod-product-compliance
Lightning Source LLC
Chambersburg PA
CBHW052135070526
44585CB00017B/1836